MICRO F...

500 FANTASTIC FACTS *about*
ANIMALS

CLARE HIBBERT

ARCTURUS

This edition published in 2018 by Arcturus Publishing Limited
26/27 Bickels Yard, 151–153 Bermondsey Street,
London SE1 3HA

Author: Clare Hibbert @ Hollow Pond
Designer: Amy McSimpson @ Hollow Pond
Editors: Clare Hibbert @ Hollow Pond and Joe Harris
Illustrator: Jake McDonald
Supplementary Artworks: Shutterstock
Science Consultant: Thomas Canavan

ISBN: 978-1-78428-796-2
CH005648NT
Supplier 29, Date 0418, Print run 6856

Printed in China

CONTENTS

1 Animal Bodies.. 4

Find out about hollow bird bones, weird frog skin, and the secret of a camel's hump!

2 Animal Habitats... 54

Marvel at birds with edible nests, as well as a beautiful habitat made entirely of skeletons!

3 On the Move.. 104

Check out the highest jumpers, the fastest fliers, and reptiles that run on water!

4 Senses and Communication................. 154

Discover creatures with mirrored eyes and star-shaped noses ... and the noisiest animals!

5 Friends and Enemies.............................. 204

Who's at the top of the food chain? Who are BFFs? And who's for dinner?

6 Babies and Homes.................................... 254

Find out about dads that get pregnant ... and creatures that never grow up!

Index... 302

A BLUE WHALE'S HEART
WEIGHS AS MUCH AS A LION

The blue whale is the biggest animal ever to have lived on Earth. It can be 110 ft (33.5 m)—as long as 18 scuba divers end to end.

A blue whale's heart weighs 400 lb (180 kg).

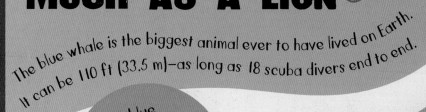

Blue whales live up to 90 years.

Weightless in water

A blue whale reaches 200 tons (181 tonnes)—the same as 28 African elephants. Its tongue alone weighs as much as one elephant. The water supports the whale's weight.

Blue whales are one of the loudest animals. Their call measures 188 decibels.

4

Some mammals weigh less than a sugar lump

At just 0.06 oz (1.8 g), the tiny Etruscan shrew is the world's lightest mammal. Its body is just 1.6 in (4 cm) long!

FAST LIVING

Small mammals often have fast heart rates, and the Etruscan shrew is no different. Its heart beats up to 1,500 times a minute—more than ten times faster than yours!

Smaller still

The bumblebee bat weighs 0.01 oz (0.2 g) more than an Etruscan shrew, but its skull is a fraction smaller.

GREEDY!

The Etruscan shrew eats almost twice its own body weight in worms and grubs every day!

5

OSTRICHES DON'T BURY
their heads in the sand

There's a saying that the ostrich buries its head, meaning it ignores danger. In fact, the world's biggest bird usually runs from any threat.

FACE PLANT

If running is not an option, an ostrich throws itself on the ground. Its head and neck blend in with the sand, but its big body is still visible!

BIGGER BIRD

Weighing up to 600 lb (275 kg), the elephant bird was even bigger than the ostrich. It lived on Madagascar until 500 years ago.

Ostriches are too heavy to fly. Males grow to 346 lb (156 kg)—as much as a sumo wrestler.

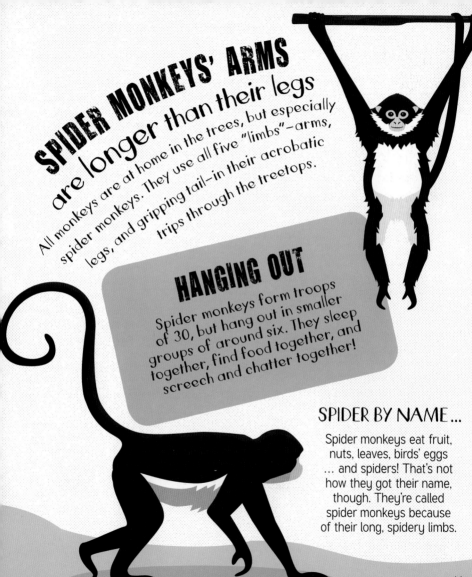

SPIDER MONKEYS' ARMS
are longer than their legs

All monkeys are at home in the trees, but especially spider monkeys. They use all five "limbs"—arms, legs, and gripping tail—in their acrobatic trips through the treetops.

HANGING OUT

Spider monkeys form troops of 30, but hang out in smaller groups of around six. They sleep together, find food together, and screech and chatter together!

SPIDER BY NAME...

Spider monkeys eat fruit, nuts, leaves, birds' eggs ... and spiders! That's not how they got their name, though. They're called spider monkeys because of their long, spidery limbs.

11

AMAZING PRIMATES

The primate family includes apes, monkeys, lemurs, and tarsiers.

The endangered golden lion tamarin is named for its lionlike mane. It lives in Brazil.

golden lion tamarin

Chimpanzees, gorillas, orangutans, gibbons, and humans are all apes! Monkeys have tails and apes do not.

chimpanzee

mandrill

The male mandrill has a blue and red face and a pink bottom. It is the biggest monkey and lives in African rain forests.

Chimpanzees are our closest animal relatives. We share more than 98% of our DNA with them!

12

Orangutans are the only large apes in Asia. They live on the islands of Borneo and Sumatra and are the biggest tree-dwelling mammals.

proboscis monkey

orangutan

The male proboscis monkey has an enormous nose. It can grow as long as 4 in (10.2 cm)!

Orangutans are the kings of the swingers! Their arms can stretch 7 ft (2 m) fingertip to fingertip.

ring-tailed lemurs

gorilla

A ring-tailed lemur baby clings to its mother's chest for the first two weeks of life. Then it rides on her back!

Gorillas are the largest primates. They spend most of the time on the ground, but sleep in nests in the trees.

INSECT SKELETONS
ARE ON THE OUTSIDE

A framework of bones—your skeleton—holds your body together. Insects don't have a skeleton. Instead, they have a tough outer case called an exoskeleton.

GROWING UP

As an insect grows, it becomes too big for its exoskeleton—but that's not a problem! It wriggles out of the old case and leaves it behind. There's a shiny new exoskeleton underneath.

CREEPY-CRAWLIES

Insects include beetles, bugs, flies, bees, butterflies, and grasshoppers. In their adult form, they all have three pairs of legs and three parts to their body. Woodlice have too many legs to be insects, but they do have exoskeletons.

14

There are more
SPINELESS ANIMALS
THAN BONY ONES

Animals that don't have spines or other inside bones are called invertebrates. More than 97% of all the animals on Earth are invertebrates!

wasp

spider

butterfly

beetle

snail

centipede

mussel

fly

SPINELESS SPECIFICATIONS

There are six groups of invertebrates:
- arthropods (insects, spiders, and crustaceans)
- jellyfish, corals, and sea anemones
- starfish, sea cucumbers, and sea urchins
- mollusks (snails, slugs, squid, and octopuses)
- segmented worms
- sponges

Amazing arthropods

The biggest arthropod is the Japanese crab, with an arm span of 12.5 ft (3.8 m). Arthropods live on land, in fresh water, and in the sea. They all have jointed legs and a tough exoskeleton.

starfish

sea urchin

octopus

Birdwings are the
BIGGEST BUTTERFLIES

The world's largest butterfly is the Queen Alexandra's birdwing, which only just fits on a large dinner plate. Its wingspan is up to 1 ft (30 cm).

male Goliath birdwing

male Cairns birdwing

FLAPPING FLIERS

The birdwings are a kind of swallowtail butterfly, famous for their wing shape, size, and birdlike flight. Females are dull brown, but males are brighter shades.

UNDER THREAT

Birdwings are endangered. Collectors took many of them from the wild. The main threat now is that the tropical forests in Southeast Asia and Australia where they live are being cut down.

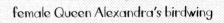

female Queen Alexandra's birdwing

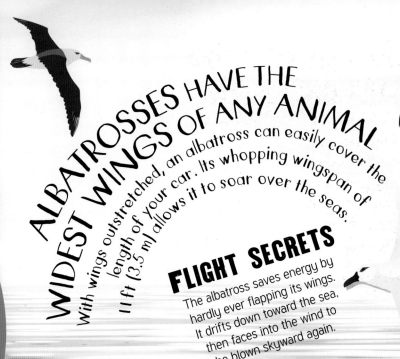

ALBATROSSES HAVE THE WIDEST WINGS OF ANY ANIMAL

With wings outstretched, an albatross can easily cover the length of your car. Its whopping wingspan of 11 ft (3.5 m) allows it to soar over the seas.

FLIGHT SECRETS

The albatross saves energy by hardly ever flapping its wings. It drifts down toward the sea, then faces into the wind to be blown skyward again.

GIANTS OF THE PAST

Some past flyers were even larger than the albatross. Prehistoric seabird *Pelagornis*'s wings measured 24 ft (7.3 m) tip to tip.

Quetzalcoatlus,
a large pterosaur

17

BIRDS HAVE
HOLLOW BONES

rainbow
bee-eater

breastbone

Birds' bones have a special feature that helps them fly—they contain a lot of air!

DESIGNED FOR FLIGHT

Like planes, birds need to be strong but light. Their bones are stiff and dense for strength. To keep their weight down, the bones have hollow pockets.

frigate
bird

A frigate bird's skeleton weighs less than its feathers!

Strong support

Many birds have a structure like a ship's keel on their breastbone. It supports the big, powerful muscles they need for flying. Flightless birds, such as ostriches, do not have this breastbone.

black-naped
oriole

MICE HAVE AS MANY NECK BONES AS GIRAFFES

The giraffe has the longest neck in the animal kingdom, at around 6 ft (1.8 m) long. However, just seven neck bones support its length.

Male giraffes bash each other's necks when they want to impress a female.

BONY BLUEPRINT

Almost every mammal—from mice to giraffes and anteaters to humans—has seven neck bones. Each giraffe neck bone is around 10 in (25.4 cm) long.

Birds have more neck bones than many other animals—up to 25 of them.

19

SOME STARFISH
HAVE 40 ARMS

The best-known starfish have five arms, but some have up to 40. "Sea stars" is a better name than "starfish," because these weird and wonderful creatures are definitely not fish!

blue sea star

Undersea survivor

There are around 2,000 different species of sea star and they live all over the world. Their average life span is about 35 years!

EYE SPY

The sea star has a simple eye at the end of each arm. It can't see well, but its limited vision helps keep it close to home.

common starfish

morning sun star

royal starfish

cushion sea star

millipede

Millipedes don't really HAVE A THOUSAND FEET

Their name means "1,000 feet," but most millipedes have between 80 and 400 legs. They have two pairs per body segment, and they grow new segments (and legs!) as they age.

LEGGIEST ANIMAL

One rare millipede, from California, has up to 750 legs! They must be very tiny because the critter's body is only 1 in (3 cm) long.

PREDATORY COUSINS

Millipedes are vegetarians, but their cousins, the centipedes, are hunters. "Centipede" means "100 legs," but they can have between 30 and 350 legs. Their bodies are flatter than millipedes'.

centipede

A PYTHON'S JAW IS ELASTICATED

A snake doesn't chew its food—it swallows it whole! It stretches its jaw to accommodate super-sized meals, such as a pig, antelope, or person!

Burmese pythons grow up to 23 ft (7 m) long.

SEE YOU LATER, ALLIGATOR

In 2015, scientists X-rayed a python that had eaten an alligator. It took three days to break down the soft tissue. After a week it had digested the skeleton and skin.

WHAT MAKES THE PYTHON'S JAW SO SPECIAL?

1) It isn't stuck firmly to the skull

2) It has two pieces, joined by stretchy ligament, and the halves can open apart

Hummingbirds
SIP THROUGH STRAWS

A hummingbird's long, pointy beak looks like a drinking straw. The bird seems to slurp nectar through it.

Hummingbirds eat half of their body weight in sugar every day!

LAPPING IT UP

The hummingbird, however, doesn't really suck up the sugary nectar—it laps it. Inside the beak, its fringed, forked tongue unfurls to grab nectar, then curls up again to carry it into the bird's mouth!

SWORD AT THE READY

The sword-billed hummingbird has a beak longer than its body. Its beak can be 4 in (10 cm) long.

chipmunk

Rodents' teeth never STOP GROWING

To stop themselves from having longer fangs than Dracula, rodents must wear down their incisor teeth with constant gnawing. Their name comes from the Latin word rodere, "to gnaw!"

red squirrel

GREAT AND SMALL

Rodents include rats, chipmunks, squirrels, and beavers. The largest is the capybara, which looks like a giant guinea pig. It grows up to 4.4 ft (1.3 m) long. The smallest rodents, the pygmy jerboa and the pygmy mouse, are around 2 in (5 cm) long, excluding their tails.

mouse

Arctic hare

capybara

ALL RELATIVES

Rabbits, hares, and pikas aren't rodents, but they are close cousins. Their incisor teeth never stop growing either!

NOT ALL ELEPHANTS HAVE TUSKS

All African elephants have tusks, but only some Asian males have them. Tusks are extra-long incisor teeth.

African elephants have larger ears, shaped like the African continent. Asian elephants have smaller ears.

Asian elephant

African elephant

The longest mammoth tusks were 16 ft (4.8 m). Mastodons were prehistoric relatives of elephants and mammoths. Their tusks were even larger—nearly 16.4 ft (5 m) long!

TUSK TASKS

Elephants use their tusks to battle enemies, dig, and forage. Tusks never stop growing and can be 12 ft (3.5 m) or more.

25

SKIN, SCALES, FUR, AND FEATHERS

Most mammals have fur or hair, but not the dolphin. Its skin is smooth and rubbery.

dolphin

A dolphin replaces its outermost layer of skin every two hours.

The raccoon has a black "mask" of fur around its eyes–like a bandit!

raccoon

Despite their name, red foxes are not always red. They can be golden, reddish-brown, black, or silver.

ocelot

Harp seals have silver fur, but their pups are pure white.

Twice the size of a house cat, the ocelot has dappled fur.

harp seal pup

Some weasels are hunted for their fur. They include the slinky brown mink and fluffy white ermine.

weasel

A reptile's dry, scaly skin helps to keep in moisture—useful in habitats that don't have much rain.

Protected today, snowy egrets were once hunted for their plumes, which decorated women's hats.

Snake skin is used for bags and shoes—but the only place it looks beautiful is on a living snake!

spotted cat snake

Raggiana bird-of-paradise

snowy egret

Male birds-of-paradise have spectacular plumage for attracting a mate.

27

CROCODILES CRY
WHEN THEY EAT

A crocodile's eyes produce moisture all the time, including when it is eating.

crocodile

EYE, EYE!

Fluid constantly flows from a crocodile's tear ducts and it does an important job. It cleans and protects the eyes so that they don't dry up. It's not a sign that the crocodile feels sorry for its victim!

sea turtle

Sharks have salt glands in their bottoms!

great white shark

Salt glands

Sea turtles "cry" to get rid of some of the sea salt in their bodies. Their salt gland is near their eyes.

A CHAMELEON'S TONGUE IS TWICE ITS BODY LENGTH

Chameleons are best known as masters of disguise, but they have another extraordinary feature–their tongue.

If your teacher's tongue were twice his or her body length, it'd be 10-12 ft (3-3.6 m) long!

IN A FLASH!

A chameleon sits motionless for hours. When it spots insect prey, it shoots out its long, sticky tongue. The tongue is back in its mouth– along with the meal–too fast for the eye to see!

SUPER SPEEDY

If the chameleon's tongue were a car, it could accelerate from 0 to 60 mph (96.6 kph) in one hundredth of a second.

THE WORLD'S BIGGEST SPIDER EATS SNAKES!

The Goliath bird-eating spider is the world's biggest spider. It has an 11-in (28-cm) leg span and weighs up to 6.2 oz (175 g).

WORM FOOD

Despite their name, Goliath bird-eating spiders mostly eat invertebrates, mice, frogs, and lizards. However, they can take bigger prey, including snakes and birds.

SPEEDY HUNTER

The giant huntsman spider has a smaller body than the Goliath bird-eater, and longer legs. These help it to run down fast-moving prey, such as cockroaches or other spiders.

Goliath bird-eating spider

earthworm

Snakes have the
STRETCHIEST BODIES

Snakes have such twisty-turny bodies that it's hard to imagine they have any bones at all!

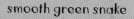

smooth green snake

In fact, snakes are bendy and flexible because they have so many bones—400 or more, compared to just 206 in adult humans.

BIG BELLY

The snake's throat makes up the front third of its body. The rest is mostly its stomach and digestive system.

The longest snake is the reticulated python. It can grow to 25 ft (7.6 m) or more.

yellow snake

The largest bats
ARE FOXES

Flying foxes are the world's largest bats. They are named for their doglike faces, and are not actually related to foxes.

The largest flying fox has a wingspan of around 6 ft (1.8 m).

FRUIT BATS

Flying foxes live in tropical rain forests in Asia, Australasia, and East Africa. Unlike small bat species, they don't have sonar. They use sight and smell to find food—nectar, flowers, pollen, and fruit.

The Indian flying fox weighs up to 3.5 lb (1.6 kg)—the same as a small Chihuahua!

The smallest flying fox species weighs just 1.5 lb (750 g).

SOME FOXES HAVE
LONGER EARS THAN RABBITS

The fennec fox is only about the same size as a wild rabbit, but its ears are much bigger!

Desert home

The fennec fox lives in the deserts of North Africa and the Middle East. Its large ears—up to 6 in (15.2 cm) long—stop it from overheating. They can also pick up the faintest sounds, helping the fox to hunt insects, rodents, eggs, and reptiles.

Eagle owls hunt fennec foxes!

HIDING FROM HEAT

Fennecs hunt at night, when it is cooler. During the daytime, they stay underground in their burrow.

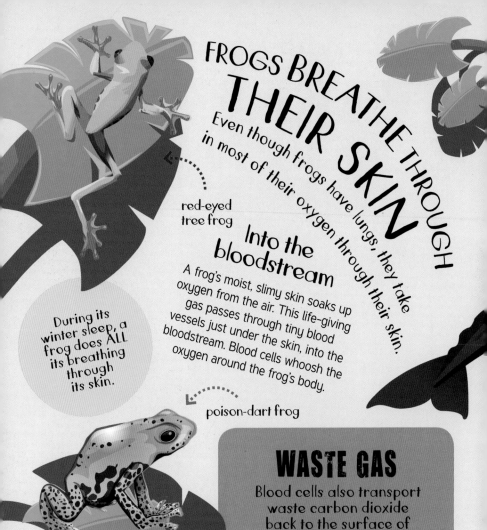

FROGS BREATHE THROUGH THEIR SKIN

Even though frogs have lungs, they take in most of their oxygen through their skin.

red-eyed tree frog

Into the bloodstream

A frog's moist, slimy skin soaks up oxygen from the air. This life-giving gas passes through tiny blood vessels just under the skin, into the bloodstream. Blood cells whoosh the oxygen around the frog's body.

During its winter sleep, a frog does ALL its breathing through its skin.

poison-dart frog

WASTE GAS

Blood cells also transport waste carbon dioxide back to the surface of the frog's skin. This gas is released back into the air.

SPERM WHALES HOLD THEIR BREATH FOR 90 MINUTES

Sperm whales hold the record for the longest, deepest dives of any mammal.

Deep breaths

All marine mammals must come to the surface to breathe air. Sperm whales can stay underwater for as long as an hour-and-a-half and dive to depths of 3,280 ft (999.7 m). They feed on giant squid.

PROTEIN POWER

Deep-diving mammals have extra helpings of myoglobin in their muscles. It's a special protein that stores oxygen.

harp seal

SOME MARINE MAMMALS

Whales
Sea lions
Dolphins

Sea otters
Seals
Polar bears

OCEAN LIFE

Oceans cover two-thirds of Earth and contain more than half its life.

sea otter

Unlike other marine mammals, a sea otter has no fatty blubber to keep it warm.

There are more than 20,000 species of fish.

flat fish

Most coral reefs grow in warm, tropical waters.

coral

angelfish

Angelfish are reef fish. They eat both plants and animals.

jellyfish

There are more than 4,000 species of jellyfish. None have brains!

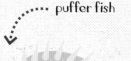

puffer fish

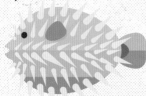

The puffer fish puffs up its body to frighten away predators.

The smallest jellyfish, the Irukandji jellyfish, is only 0.98 in (2.5 cm), but its venom can kill a person.

The sea cucumber is related to sea stars and sea urchins—not the cucumber plant!

eel

sea cucumber

Eels are fish. There are more than 400 species of eel.

A whale shark's mouth
IS 5 FT (1.5 M) WIDE

The whale shark is the largest fish in the sea. It is about as long as a bus!

FILTER FEEDER

Most sharks are fierce hunters, but the whale shark is a filter feeder. It takes in huge gulps of seawater, which it "sieves" for tiny creatures called plankton.

A whale shark weighs around 20.6 tons (18.7 tonnes).

Although big, a whale shark is still only about a third as long as a blue whale.

OCEAN SUNFISH ARE THE
HEAVIEST BONY FISH

Averaging 2,000 lb (900 kg), the ocean sunfish is pretty big... And the largest one on record was two-and-a-half times that!

BATHING BEAUTY

Ocean sunfish sunbathe at the surface, lying on their side. Maybe it warms them up after deep diving for jellyfish!

BONY OR NOT?

About 90% of all the fish in the oceans are bony fish, like the ocean sunfish. That means they have proper bone, not bendy cartilage like sharks and rays.

SO GOOD THEY NAMED IT TWICE...

The ocean sunfish's Latin name is Mola mola!

A CAMEL'S HUMP DOES NOT STORE WATER

Humps help a camel to survive in the desert because they store fat.

dromedary camel

ONE HUMP OR TWO?

Camels can turn the fat back into energy. Most camels are dromedaries, with one hump. Bactrian camels live in Central Asia and have two humps.

DESERT-PROOF FEATURES OF CAMELS

✓ fatty hump

✓ not losing much water as sweat or urine

✓ double row of eyelashes to keep out sand

✓ wide feet to spread their weight

Bactrian camel

Ships of the desert

Desert people have kept camels for 5,000 years. As well as being strong, hardy pack animals, they provide milk, meat, and hair for making textiles.

RHINO HORNS
NEVER STOP GROWING

Rhinoceros horns are made from keratin, just like your hair and fingernails.

ONE HORN OR TWO?

White and black rhinos live in Africa and have two horns. Indian and Javan rhinos have one horn, just 22 in (55 cm). The rare Sumatran rhino has two, but one is very short and stubby.

HORN HERO

The longest rhino horn was 5 ft (1.5 m) long. It belonged to a white rhino.

Horns are a bit like EXTREMELY matted hair!

During the Ice Age, herds of woolly rhinos roamed Europe and northern Asia.

Snakes shed
THEIR SKIN

All snakes, large
and small, peel
off their skin,
leaving behind
a ghostly shell.

SCALE TALE

A snake's skin is made up of small, overlapping scales. Scales are tough, but after a few months' wear and tear they need replacing. The old skin splits to reveal a shiny new skin underneath!

coral snake

Iguanas and other lizards
shed their skin in patches, not
all in one piece like snakes.

Crocodiles' scales are
tough and plate-like. They're
replaced one at a time.

Most turtles don't shed their
skin. Instead, they grow a new
layer under their shell.

SOME WOLVES HAVE MANES

Is it a fox? Is it a wolf? No, it's a maned wolf—the largest wild dog in South America.

Fox on stilts

The maned wolf is very tall, thanks to its super-long legs. Most of its fur is red, like a fox's. When it senses danger, the long, black fur on the back of the maned wolf's neck stands on end.

EWW!

The maned wolf has very smelly pee—that's why it's nicknamed the "skunk wolf!"

Most hyenas have manes, too.

PERFECT PETS

The first domesticated animal was the dog. Humans tamed the wolf around 30,000 years ago.

Great Dane

The Great Dane is the tallest dog breed, standing 30 in (76 cm) at the shoulder.

More than a third of US households have a pet dog.

Persian cat

Chihuahua

The Chihuahua is the smallest dog breed. The tiniest ones stand less than 4 in (10 cm).

The Persian is the most popular cat breed in the US.

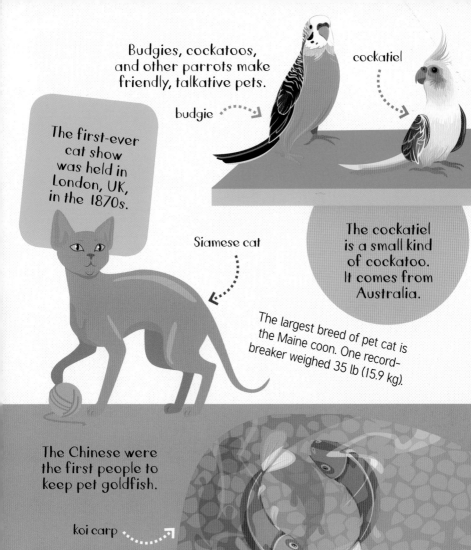

Budgies, cockatoos, and other parrots make friendly, talkative pets.

cockatiel

budgie

The first-ever cat show was held in London, UK, in the 1870s.

Siamese cat

The cockatiel is a small kind of cockatoo. It comes from Australia.

The largest breed of pet cat is the Maine coon. One record-breaker weighed 35 lb (15.9 kg).

The Chinese were the first people to keep pet goldfish.

koi carp

45

SOME ALPACAS HAVE
DREADLOCKS

There are just two breeds of alpaca. Huacayas have a thick, fluffy fleece and are the most popular. Suris have long, wavy hair that clumps together in corded dreadlocks!

WILD BEGINNINGS

Alpacas look like small llamas. Their ancestors are the wild vicunas that live in the Andes Mountains of South America. People spin alpaca hair into beautifully soft ponchos, blankets, sweaters, hats, and more!

SPITTING MAD

Like their cousins, the camels, alpacas are known for being bad-tempered. They spit at other alpacas to keep competitors away from food and warn away aggressors.

46

Echidna spines
ARE JUST WEIRD HAIRS

Also called spiny anteaters, echidnas are funny-looking creatures, covered in prickly spines.

All four echidna species live in Australia, Tasmania, and New Guinea.

PROTECTIVE COATING

Echidnas' spines evolved (developed slowly over time) from their hairy coats. Ones with thick, spiky hairs were more likely to deter predators. Echidnas curl into a ball so an attacker faces a prickly mouthful.

Mammal misfits

Echidnas lay eggs instead of having live babies. They are more closely related to the duck-billed platypus—the only other egg-laying mammal—than to spine-covered hedgehogs or porcupines.

Giraffes get by on
HARDLY ANY SLEEP

An adult giraffe has just 15 to 30 minutes of sleep in any 24-hour period.

Lions, the main predators in the giraffe's grassland home, sleep for 20 hours per day.

EVER READY

The giraffe naps for a minute or two at a time, either standing up or lying down. It takes this spindly giant time to get up from the floor, so it snoozes with one eye open, watching for danger.

A SIMILAR TRICK

How do dolphins swim and come up for air, but also sleep? They shut down one side of their brain at a time, including the eye it controls.

48

SLOTHS ARE NOT
THE SLEEPIEST ANIMALS

The sloth has such a reputation for snoozing that even its name means "laziness!"

Giant armadillos sleep a lot, too— for as much as 18 hours per day.

Yawny koala

Sloths sleep for 20 hours a day, but Australia's koala sleeps for 22 hours! Its diet doesn't help. The koala eats only eucalyptus leaves, which take a very long time to digest.

PROCESSING POWER

Koalas eat about 2.5 lb (1.1 kg) of eucalyptus a day. The leaves must travel along its 6.6-ft (2-m) gut, which is more than three times the animal's body length!

Lizards "DROP" THEIR TAILS

Lizards have a neat trick for distracting predators—they let the end of their tail fall off.

DAZZLING DECOY

And that's not all! The tail wriggles, flips, and tumbles long after it's detached from the body. Hopefully it holds the predator's attention while the lizard makes its getaway.

SAVING ENERGY

The tail moves about so much that the predator cannot catch it. When the coast is clear, the lizard may come back and eat its own tail. Sounds gross? It means the lizard can get back some of the energy it lost. It'll need it to regrow its tail.

CREATURES REGROW BODY PARTS

The axolotl, a kind of salamander, is a champion regenerator. It can replace a tail or leg, and even mend its own heart or brain!

When an earthworm is cut in two, the half with its head can regrow a tail.

A spiny mouse can completely heal wounds or grow back missing skin in record time!

A sea star can regrow any arm that breaks off!

A deer can regrow 60 lb (27 kg) of antlers in just three months!

SPIDER SILK IS
stronger than steel

Bridges aren't built from silk just yet, however...

STRENGTHS AND WEAKNESSES

Spider silk cannot take quite as much stress as steel before it breaks. But the silk is so much less dense than steel that it wins out. It is five times stronger than the same weight of steel.

A spider uses body parts called spinnerets to shape the silk.

VERSATILE SILK

Spiders make their silk from proteins. They use it for many jobs, including building webs, protecting eggs, ballooning through the air, and wrapping up their prey like mummies.

Female golden orb spiders produce golden silk.

black widow spider

THE LARGEST PEARL ISN'T ROUND

The biggest known pearl is pillow-sized and weighs as much as an adult Labrador Retriever.

Not all pearls are natural. Some are made in factories.

ONE FOR LUCK

The record-breaking pearl belonged to a fisherman from the Philippine Islands, who used to touch it for luck. Worth more than $100 million, the pearl had formed inside a giant clam shell.

How irritating!

Oysters, clams, and mussels all produce pearls if grit gets inside their shell. Their body covers the object with thin, pearly layers so it cannot irritate them. Pearls chosen for jewels are often perfectly round.

There are more than
EIGHT MILLION ANIMAL
SPECIES ON EARTH

Many animals live in just one particular kind of place, or habitat. Earth has many different habitats. There are ...

mountains

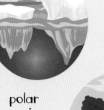

polar regions

oceans

deserts

grasslands

rain forests

... and more!

JUST RIGHT

Animals adapt to their habitat so that it's just right. They can cope with its climate and weather. They eat the plants that grow there or the other animals that live there.

The polar bear's icy habitat is the region around the North Pole.

EARTH HAS
DEAD ZONES

Is all of Earth's surface a habitat for animals? Not at all! Some places have no life.

There are vast areas of the ocean where nothing really lives. Other places are lifeless because of human actions.

Pollution from factories can destroy habitats.

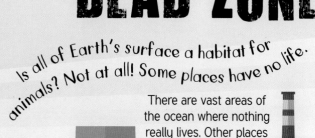

ALGAE ATTACK

Coastal areas can be dead zones because they have TOO MUCH life! Algae grows monstrously well where fertilizer has run off farm fields into rivers and then the sea. The algae blocks out the light and uses up oxygen. No fish or other marine life can survive.

HALF OF THE WORLD'S ANIMALS LIVE IN RAIN FORESTS

Tropical rain forests are excellent habitats. They are warm and wet, and there is lush plant life.

SPECIES IN THE AMAZON

1,300 birds

scarlet macaw

430+ mammals

spider monkey

poison-dart frog

400+ reptiles

400+ amphibians

More than 100 species of poison-dart frog live in the Amazon.

green tree snake

3,000 fish

piranha

Totally tropical

Tropical rain forests grow near the equator, the imaginary line around the middle of the Earth. The Amazon in South America is the largest rain forest. It rains there nearly every day and the temperature is around 80 °F (27 °C).

56

One tree hosts HUNDREDS OF SPECIES

The tallest trees in the rain forest are 200 ft (60.9 m) high. The tree is a home, lookout post, nursery, and food source to countless creatures.

LAYERS OF LIFE

One tree can feed hundreds of plant-eaters with its leaves, bark, sap, fruit, and seeds. In turn, these monkeys, birds, and insects feed snakes, jaguars, and other predators.

.... emergent layer

ANT-TASTIC

One rain forest tree can contain more than 40 kinds of ant—that's more ant species than live in the whole of the British Isles!

.... canopy

.... understory

leafcutter ants

.... forest floor

Sloths do (almost) everything upside down...

Sloths are super-cute mammals that live in rain forest trees in Central and South America.

WHICH WAY'S UP?

Sloths spend most of their time hanging upside down. They appear motionless but are actually moving very, very slowly. Their long, strong claws grip the tree branches.

RIGHT WAY UP

Sloths come down to the forest floor once a week and stand the right way up to poop and urinate. That doesn't sound like very often, but sloths' digestive systems are slow, too!

SOME LIZARDS "FLY"

The Draco lizard has winglike flaps on the sides of its body. It's not capable of powered flight, but it can glide from tree to tree.

Draco lizard

flying gecko

flying frog

FEET FIRST

Flying frogs stay airborne thanks to extra webbing between their toes. They spread them out to catch the air.

RAIN FOREST GLIDERS

All 42 species of *Draco* lizard can glide as far as 200 ft (60 m). Their "wing" membranes are supported on extra-long ribs that stick out from the body. Flying geckos follow a different design—their "wings" are flaps joining their limbs and body.

DEER LIVE
IN ALL KINDS OF
FORESTS

There are different kinds of forest habitat, and different species of deer live in them.

Reindeer (caribou) and moose (elk) roam the **taiga**–forests of conifers in the far north of Europe, Asia, and America that have very cold winters.

Small deer species, including brocket deer and muntjacs, live in **tropical rain forests**.

Red deer inhabit **temperate woodlands**. There are four seasons and the trees are deciduous (they lose their leaves).

The tiniest deer is the southern pudu, from the **temperate rain forests** of Chile and Argentina.

WOLVERINES

PREFER FARAWAY FORESTS

Habitats can be close to people and settlements or remote and hard to reach. Wolverines live far from humans in the taiga.

taiga (green)

TAIGA-PROOF FEATURES OF WOLVERINES

✓ oily, frost-proof fur

✓ not too fussy to scavenge when food is scarce

✓ long claws for strong grip on icy ground

SHY AND SOLITARY

Wolverines aren't related to wolves or comic-book characters, but they ARE very fierce and strong! These animal outcasts from the weasel family look like small bears.

Wolverines mark their territory with such a stinky smell that they are nicknamed "skunk bears!"

URBAN ANIMALS

Urban animals need their wits about them. Some have bigger brains than their country cousins!

Coyotes and raccoons scavenge and hunt across North America in many habitats, including towns and cities.

House geckos keep insects under control by eating them. How helpful! However, they're also a nuisance because they poop everywhere!

There are about a dozen species of fox. The red fox is the largest, and the most common in cities.

The red fox is found in more places around the world than any other carnivore (meat-eater).

There are 400 million rock pigeons in cities worldwide.

Pigeons are small but deadly. They carry microbes such as *Salmonella*, *Listeria*, and *Cryptococcus*, which causes a life-threatening form of meningitis.

Macaques living in Southeast Asian countries have become skilled pickpockets!

Black rats spread the Black Death, or plague, that killed up to 100 million people during the 1300s.

New York City has around two million rats, mostly brown ones.

Grassland grazers
LIVE IN HERDS

There aren't many hiding places in open grassland. The plant-eating animals that live there group together in herds for safety.

gazelle

SAVANNA

Many plant-eaters live on the African savanna, including gazelles. They face lions, hyenas, and cheetahs.

HUGE HERDS

Wildebeest are always on the move in search of new grass and water. Sometimes they form mixed herds with zebras.

zebra

CONFUSING!

A zebra's dazzling stripes make it hard for a lion or hyena to pick off an individual animal from the herd.

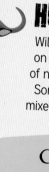

wildebeest

WATER DEER DON'T LIVE IN WATER

Ponds, rivers, and lakes are freshwater habitats. All sorts of animals live in and around them. Water deer live alongside rivers, not IN them!

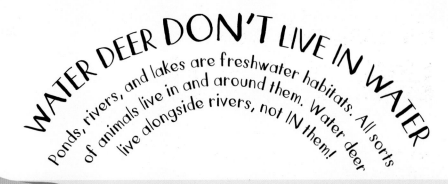

NOW DUCK!

Ducks nest along riverbanks, but spend most of the day out on the water. They dive for waterweed, insects, mollusks, and fish. Male ducks often have bright, showy feathers.

mallard

mandarin duck

trout

FRESHWATER FISH

Tench, trout, perch, and pike are all freshwater fish. Life is a challenge for fish in ponds. In summer, the pond might dry up; in winter, there is the risk of freezing.

pike

Hippos wear
SUNSCREEN

Hippopotamuses live in sub-Saharan Africa. They wallow in rivers all day to keep cool, but they still need protection from the hot sun's dangerous rays.

SUPER SWEAT!

Hippos ooze oily, reddish-orange "sweat" from pores in their skin. It contains chemicals that soak up dangerous ultraviolet (UV) light—the rays that damage skin. The sweat is antibacterial too, so it stops wounds from getting infected.

BLOOD RED

People used to believe that hot hippos would sweat blood!

SOME WHALES TAN... AND SOME DON'T.

blue whale

Blue whales spend their winter vacations in the sunnier seas around Mexico. Their skin reacts to the extra UV light—it produces darker pigments, just like human skin when it tans.

fin whale

DARK BEGINNINGS

Fin whales are different. They are naturally darker-skinned than blue whales because they have a pigment called melanin in their skin. The melanin protects against the sun.

BASKERS

Sperm whales spend up to six hours at a time basking at the surface. Their skin contains proteins that help it to avoid UV damage.

sperm whale

67

OLMS
WERE THE FIRST
CAVE CREATURES
SCIENTISTS STUDIED

Cool, dark, and damp, caves are a habitat for some crazy creatures, such as the olm. This salamander was described and given its scientific name way back in 1768.

Cave senses

The olm is blind, but sight isn't that useful in its dark home. It has excellent senses of smell, hearing, and touch. In times of plenty, an olm stores up enough sugars to survive ten years without food!

FIVE FREAKY CAVE CRITTERS

Cave cricket

Cave spider

Cave crayfish

Cave fish

Cave salamander

small, useless legs

large head

snakelike, slithering body

frilly gills for underwater breathing

One can house MILLIONS OF BATS

Bats are probably the best-known cave dwellers. Many species roost in damp, dark caves during the day.

Free-tailed bats are about 3.7 in (9.5 cm) long. Half of that is tail.

BAT NURSERY

Every year, around ten million Mexican free-tailed bats fly to Bracken Cave in Texas to give birth. For the first four or five weeks of life, the baby bats feed only on mother's milk. They suckle from their mothers' armpits!

PRECIOUS POOP

Millions of bats produce plenty of poop. It's stinky, but it's also an important food for bacteria, fungi, and even salamanders. Yum!

guano (bat poop)

SHEEP ARE SURE-FOOTED

Wild sheep live in hills and mountains. If they weren't steady on their feet, they'd always be slipping on loose rocks or tripping over cliffs.

MADE FOR MOUNTAINS

Sheep have thick, woolly hair to keep out the cold. They huddle together in flocks for warmth and as a protection against wolves and other mountain predators.

bighorn sheep

mountain goat

GOATS VS SHEEP

Wild goats and wild sheep are related, but they're not the same. Wild sheep are larger and have thicker horns. Wild goats are native to North America, while wild sheep come from Asia.

Yaks have BIG LUNGS

Yaks are wild cattle from the Himalayas. Extra-large lungs help them survive in their harsh habitat.

BREATHING DEEP

At high altitudes, the air's thinner and contains less oxygen. Thanks to its big lungs, the yak takes in more air with each breath. It also has an extra-high count of red blood cells—the ones that carry oxygen around the body.

There are more than 12 million domestic yaks, but only around 10,000 wild ones.

WINTER SURVIVAL

Yaks' shaggy coats help them to survive temperatures as low as -40 °F (-40 °C). In winter, yaks eat snow to keep themselves hydrated.

FARM
ANIMALS

Sheep and goats were the first animals tamed to be a source of food, around 11,000 years ago.

Early people tamed dogs to help them to hunt and to guard their settlements.

The tallest, heaviest horse ever was a Shire horse called Sampson. It weighed 3,360 lb (1,524 kg).

A turkey's wattle changes shade with its mood.

Goats and sheep don't have teeth in their upper jaws.

The smallest chicken is the Serama. It's less than 9.8 in (25 cm) tall.

Some chickens lay more than 300 eggs a year.

The largest pig, a Poland China called Big Bill, weighed 2,550 lb (1,157 kg).

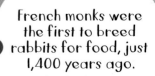

French monks were the first to breed rabbits for food, just 1,400 years ago.

ARCTIC FOXES
CHANGE COATS

That's right! Foxes are sneaky hunters because they blend in with their surroundings. They're not the only ones who dress differently in winter, either!

TUNDRA

Arctic foxes live in the Arctic tundra, a barren landscape with small plants and no trees. Tundra covers about a fifth of the land on Earth.

WINTER WHITES

Collared lemmings, hares, weasels, and foxes all change from brown to white in winter. Their paler fur helps them hide in the snowy landscape—from their predators or their prey.

Arctic foxes are the only native land mammals in Iceland!

Polar bears have
BLACK SKIN

They may look white, but polar bears actually have clear fur and their skin is black, not white!

TRICKS OF THE LIGHT

Polar bear hair looks white (even though it's clear) for four reasons:

1. Sunlight bounces inside the hollow hairs, creating a glow.
2. Teeny-tiny bumps on the hairs' surfaces scatter the light.
3. The hairs contain proteins called keratin, which are white.
4. Salt from the ocean may coat the hairs, too.

SUN SHIELD

Black skin protects the polar bear from the sun's strong UV rays, but also helps it soak up maximum heat.

Snow leopards WEAR SNOWSHOES

Snow leopards have outsized paws that spread their weight and stop them from sinking into the snow. It's as if they have their own snowshoes!

Snow leopards have an extra-long tail for balance. It is almost as long as the body!

Snow leopards have the largest leap of any cat—about ten times their own body length!

ROCKS AND RAVINES

Snow leopards live in the rugged mountains of Central Asia. Their smoky fur with black rosettes provides perfect camouflage in the rough, rocky landscape, which has snow for much of the year.

BEARS SLEEP ALL WINTER

Bears are famous for their long winter sleep, but do they hibernate? They certainly don't behave the same way as smaller hibernators.

brown bear

chipmunk

HOW TO HIBERNATE

When chipmunks or other small mammals hibernate, they lower their body temperature to just above freezing. Once a week, they wake, raise their temperature, eat stored food, and pass waste.

Special case

Bears are different—they only lower their temperature a little. This made scientists think bears weren't truly hibernating—until they looked at the bigger picture. Bears in their winter sleep can go for 100 days without eating, drinking, urinating, or pooping!

77

DESERT BIRDS
NEST IN CACTUSES

In the deserts of the
southwestern United States
and western Mexico, there
are cactuses as tall as trees.
And like trees, they're
home to nesting birds!

Builder birds

Gila woodpeckers use their strong beaks
to dig out holes in saguaro cactuses. They
have a distinctive, bright red "cap."

READY-MADE

Old woodpecker nests provide a
home for other birds, including
the cactus wren and tiny elf owl.

Elf owls are
the lightest owls.
They weigh about
the same as a slice of
bread—1.4 oz (40 g).

USEFUL CACTUS
NEST FEATURES

✓ Protective prickles

✓ Cool shade

✓ Ready supply
of insects to eat

GROUND SQUIRRELS CARRY PARASOLS

Ground squirrels are rodents related to prairie dogs. They use their tails as sunshades!

MAKING SHADOWS

All squirrels, including ground squirrels, can flick back their tail to shade their body. It lowers their temperature by up to 5 °F (3 °C)!

One prairie dog "town" in Texas was home to 400 million prairie dogs. It covered 25,000 sq miles (65,000 sq km).

ANOTHER NEAT TAIL TRICK

1 A snake approaches.

2 The prairie dog waves its tail up and down as a warning.

3 The snake detects the warning and decides not to attack.

EAGLES FISH WITH THEIR FEET

A bird's feet suit its habitat and help it to find its food.

TERRIFYING TALONS

The majestic bald eagle lives near open water. It snatches up fish and waterbirds in its talons. The claws keep a firm grip, even on slippery salmon!

WIDE WINGS

The bald eagle's powerful wings spread out 8 ft (2.3 m). Even when it is carrying a meal, the bird can fly at 30 mph (48 kph).

salmon

THREE OTHER HUGE EAGLES IN NORTH AMERICA

golden eagle
wingspan: 7.5 ft (2.3 m)

white-tailed eagle
wingspan: 8 ft (2.4 m)

Steller's sea eagle
wingspan: 8.2 ft (2.5 m)

A THORNY DEVIL
DRINKS WITH ITS FEET

This strange little lizard lives in the Australian desert.

DEWY DRINKS

The thorny devil's spikes and spines protect against predators, but the gaps between them are useful, too. Grooves all over the lizard's skin—including on its feet—soak up dew. They channel the water to the thorny devil's mouth!

The thorny devil's scientific name is Moloch horridus, after a bloodthirsty king called Moloch.

 ## Ant eaters

Thorny devils also get a little liquid, but not much, from their food. They don't have the most adventurous diet. They eat black ants, and nothing else!

ELEPHANTS USE THEIR
EARS AS FANS

It's hot all year round on the African savanna. So how does a lumbering giant stay cool?

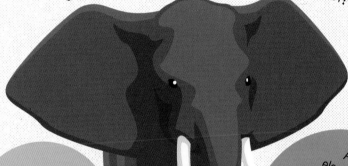

An elephant drinks up to 50 gallons (189 l) of water a day.

African elephants flap their huge ears to create a cooling draft! The flapping also gets rid of body heat, which blood vessels bring to the surface of the ears.

EAR, EAR!

Elephants spread out their ears if they feel threatened. It makes them look even bigger than they already are!

MAMMOTHS HAD SMALLER
EARS THAN ELEPHANTS

Woolly mammoths were relatives of elephants that lived
from 400,000 to 10,000 years ago, during the last Ice Age.

KEEPING OUT THE COLD

Woolly mammoths' ears were smaller than those of modern
elephants, so they lost less body heat. Mammoths
also had long, thick fur to keep out the
cold. A hump behind their head
stored fat, just like a camel's hump.

CUTE COUSIN

Woolly mammoths
stood 11 ft (3.4 m)
at the shoulder.
A dwarf species,
just half this height,
lived on Wrangel
Island, off the coast
of Siberia, until
4,000 years ago.

FRESHWATER ANIMALS

American water shrews are so light that they can walk on water!

A diving bell spider lives almost entirely under water in an air-filled web.

Most frogs can jump 30 times their own body length.

Toads lay strings of eggs up to 20-66 ft (6-20 m) long.

An electric eel can give off a charge of more than 500 volts.

A water flea is no bigger than a poppy seed.

An adult dragonfly eats hundreds of mosquitoes a day.

The largest living dragonfly is 4 in (10 cm) long with a wingspan of 7.5 in (19 cm).

Water scorpions don't sting with their long tails—they breathe through them!

Mayflies appeared more than 350 million years ago—before the dinosaurs!

85

TIDAL POOL CREATURES ARE SUPER TOUGH

Animals in tidal pools are survivors. They must adapt to changes in their environment in an instant.

QUICK CHANGE

The pool's temperature, saltiness, and oxygen levels are always changing. A rush of cold water swishes into the pool twice a day.

THE TIDE SWIRLS IN!

The barnacle's plates open and its 12 legs wave around catching plankton.

The sea anemone waves its tentacles.

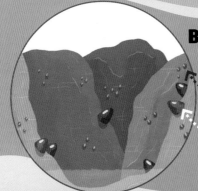

BETWEEN THE TIDES ...

The barnacle protects its body from drying with a "shell" of tight-fitting plates.

The sea anemone pulls in its tentacles.

86

WADERS WALK ON STILTS

Storks and herons are long-legged wading birds.

marabou stork

LEGGY LIFESTYLE

Storks and herons live in freshwater and coastal habitats. They wade through the water on stilt-like legs, looking for fish, crabs, and other prey.

GIANTS

At 59 in (150 cm) tall, the marabou is the largest stork. The largest heron, the Goliath heron, is a fraction taller at 59.8 in (152 cm). Both of these birds live in southern Africa.

great blue heron

WETLAND WADERS

✓ Heron   ✓ Spoonbill

✓ Stork   ✓ Crane

✓ Ibis

THE OPEN OCEAN IS A HABITAT

Far from land is the open ocean. It's a habitat, but the animals can be few and far between.

albatross

NIGHT TIME VISITORS

Some sea creatures feed near the surface at night. They include schools of herring and mackerel.

herring shoal

marlin

SPEEDY PREDATORS

Blue sharks, marlins, and makos cover long distances in search of food. They compete with seabirds. An albatross can dive as deep as 23 ft (7 m) to catch prey!

The open ocean covers more than 139 million sq miles (360 million sq km)—that's two-and-a-half times the land area of Earth.

THERE ARE CHIMNEYS UNDER THE SEA

In parts of the seabed, "chimney pots" called black smokers gush out hot water that has been heated under Earth's crust.

BUILDING A CHIMNEY

The hot water spurts out of a vent (hole) in the seabed. Grains in the water sink and pile up into chimneys around the vent. Bacteria feed on these minerals.

hot water

black smoker

giant tubeworms

CRAZY GIANTS

Giant red-and-white tubeworms are one of the creatures that feed on the bacteria around the black smokers. They can grow taller than basketball players–up to 8 ft (2.4 m).

Water gushing from a hot smoker can be up to 752 °F (400 °C)– as hot as a pizza oven!

CORAL REEFS ARE MADE OF SKELETONS

Corals are made of tiny creatures called polyps. A coral reef builds up from the rocky remains of the polyps' skeletons.

black coral

pillar coral

HOW A REEF FORMS

1 Polyps live in groups in warm, tropical seas.

2 When polyps die, their chalky skeletons are left behind.

3 Layers of skeleton build the reef up higher.

sea sponge

brain coral

Living corals come in all kinds of shapes—some even look like brains!

bubble coral

The 1,430-mile (2,300-km) Great Barrier Reef contains more than 600 types of coral.

CLOWNFISH LIVE IN
THE STINGERS

Clownfish are beautiful orange, white, and black reef fish. They have a neat trick for avoiding attention from predators.

antler coral

PROTECTIVE PETALS

Clownfish often live among anemones–strange, undersea creatures that look more like plants than animals! The waving "petals" are deadly stingers, but the clownfish has a thick layer of mucus that stops it from being stung.

Give and take

The anemone provides the fish with a safe, well-defended home. In return, the clownfish cleans the anemone's tentacles and provides it with nutrients when it poops!

BEAVERS ARE AMAZING BUILDERS

Beavers live in homes called lodges. They build these lodges in the middle of a pond.

Beavers are busiest at night.

FELLING TREES

Beavers build with logs. First they gnaw around the base of a tree with their sharp front teeth until it falls down. TIMBER! Then they chew up the trunk into logs.

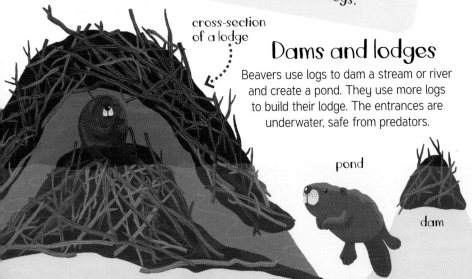

cross-section of a lodge

Dams and lodges

Beavers use logs to dam a stream or river and create a pond. They use more logs to build their lodge. The entrances are underwater, safe from predators.

pond

dam

SOME INSECTS
BUILD TOWERS

Termites live in big groups called colonies. In hot parts of Africa, Australia, and South America, termites build towering earth mounds over their nests.

There are about 2,700 known termite species.

Termite types

The REPRODUCTIVES in the colony include the king and queen, as well as any of their offspring that will grow wings and fly off to start new colonies. The WORKERS dig tunnels, repair the nest, and find food and water. SOLDIERS defend the mound.

Termite colonies live in the same mounds for centuries.

The earth helps to keep the temperature inside consistent.

93

Some birds BUILD APARTMENT BUILDINGS

Weaver birds are famous for their fancy nests. Some species build huge structures that house lots of families.

Sociable weavers' nests are the largest structures built by birds.

GIANT HAYSTACK

A sociable weaver's nest looks like a huge haystack stuck in a tree. The biggest ones have more than a hundred chambers, each housing a pair of birds.

WEAVING A NEST

Not all weavers nest together, but they all build amazing nests!

3 The bird builds an entrance passage at the bottom of the nest, too narrow for snakes or other predators to enter.

The weaver bird pulls each strip tight.

1 The weaver bird uses strands of grass or strips of leaf to make a loop.

2 The bird weaves in more strips to make a snug nest.

94

WEAVER ANTS BUILD
NESTS OF SILK

Weaver ants make a home of leaves.
They stitch them together with sticky thread.

JOINT EFFORT

The adult ants collect the leaves. They link legs to form a chain and hold the leaves in position. Adults can't make thread, but larvae can—they are pressed over the joins like glue sticks!

Weaver ants live in the tropics of Asia and Australia.

One colony can contain half a million weaver ants.

One weaver ant can hold up to 100 times its own weight.

FANTASTIC NESTS

The largest bald eagle nest, or eyrie, was 9.5 ft (2.9 m) wide and 19.7 ft (6 m) deep.

The hooded oriole often builds its nest on the underside of a palm leaf.

The Australian malleefowl's nest is a heap of rotting compost and sand. It keeps the eggs warm.

The Chinese serve up swiftlets' nests, which are made of spit, in bird's nest soup.

Gyrfalcons reuse their cliff-ledge nests. One is 2,500 years old.

The cuckoo lays its eggs in another bird's nest.

The European bee eater nests in a burrow dug out of a riverbank.

Burrowing parrots nest in cliff holes. Some colonies contain up to 70,000 birds.

The tiny tailorbird stitches leaves with plant parts to make its nest.

coot

Coots build nests on floating platforms.

Wasps make NESTS OF PAPER

Paper wasps make amazing nests that look like works of art!

CHEW AND SPIT

Paper wasps gather plant stems and tear strips of wood from trees or fences. They chew the plant material with spit to make a kind of paper.

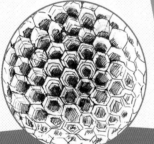

LAYERS AND LAYERS

Paper wasps build their nest with flower-like layers. It has lots of compartments for their eggs and young, or larvae.

There are about 200 species of paper wasp.

The biggest-ever wasps' nest was 22 ft (6.7 m) long and housed more than 100,000 wasps.

HUMMINGBIRD NESTS ARE
WALNUT SIZED

The world's smallest nest belongs to the tiny bee hummingbird. The nest is just 1 in (2.5 cm) wide—about the size of a walnut!

Delicate cup

Hummingbird nests are made by the females, not the males. A bee hummingbird uses cobwebs, bark, and lichen for hers. Then she lays two tiny eggs, each no bigger than a pea!

walnut

LARGEST HUMMINGBIRD

The giant hummingbird is about ten times bigger than a bee hummingbird. Her nest measures about 8 in (20 cm) across. She weaves it from grass, moss, and spider web and lines it with soft animal hair and feather down.

TURTLES HAVE MOBILE HOMES

Turtles carry their home on their back in the form of a tough shell. It shelters them from the weather and protects them from danger.

Most turtles can tuck their heads into their shells for safety.

The first turtles lived in dinosaur times, around 215 million years ago.

SHELL SHELTER

The turtle's shell is made of bone. The horned plates, or scutes, on top are made of keratin, the same material as your nails.

The flat underside of a turtle's shell is called the plastron.

The leatherback sea turtle is the world's largest turtle.

Hermit crabs borrow
THEIR HOMES

Hermit crabs don't have a hard shell like other crabs. Instead they borrow one, usually from another creature.

STRANGE SHELL SUBSTITUTES

Pen lid

Flowerpot

Soda can

Bottle cap

Old doll's head

Toy teacup

NO PLACE LIKE HOME

A hermit crab squeezes its body into an empty old shell from a sea snail or other mollusk. As the crab grows, it "moves house" into new, larger shells.

Coconut crabs live as hermit crabs for their first year or so—until their bodies become hard enough to no longer need a borrowed shell!

BURROWS KEEP ANIMALS
cool in hot places ...

Meerkats live in the Kalahari Desert. They dig underground burrows to live in.

MEERKAT PREDATORS

Jackals

Hyenas

Spitting cobras

Martial eagles

Tawny eagles

Hawks

MEERKAT MOUND

Up to 40 meerkats live in the burrow. It has many tunnels and several entrances. When the meerkats are out looking for food, one stays on watch. At any sign of danger, it barks a warning, and the whole mob rushes underground!

DESERT BURROWS

All small desert mammals live underground, from gerbils to jerboas and from gophers to badgers. The burrow protects them from the sun and from predators.

... and warm in cold places

Lemmings and ground squirrels live in the cold tundra, where the ground is frozen for much of the year.

lemming

SAFE, WARM, AND DRY

Many rodents dig underground burrows for their winter sleep or hibernation. They also use burrows as a safe, snug place to have their young.

UNDERGROUND LIFE

Some animals are especially adapted to life underground. Moles have poor sight and powerful front legs for digging. Their lungs can cope with the reduced oxygen and increased carbon dioxide underground.

hamster

UNLUCKY FOR SOME ... 13 BURROWERS

Aardvark	Groundhog
Pika	Hamster
Badger	Naked mole-rat
Prairie dog	Armadillo
Ferret	Bilby
Rabbit	Fox
Golden mole	

badger

rabbit

mole

armadillo

103

3 On the Move

THE FASTEST ANIMAL IS A
BIRD OF PREY

The peregrine falcon's average diving speed is 200 mph (322 kph)—but it can plummet as fast as 242 mph (389 kph)!

A golden eagle's average dive speed is 150 mph (241 kph).

FAST FALCONS

The gyrfalcon can outfly a peregrine falcon, although it cannot dive as fast. A peregrine's maximum is 68 mph (110 kph), while the gyrfalcon can fly at up to 90 mph (145 kph)—the same speed as a fastball in baseball!

Horizontal speeds

Homing pigeons reach speeds of 110 mph (177 kph). Swifts fly at 69 mph (112 kph).

homing pigeon

NO ANIMAL OUTRUNS A CHEETAH

The cheetah is the fastest land animal. Its top sprinting speed is more than 68 mph (100 kph).

FAST FOOD

Cheetahs have to be swift to chase their fast prey! Speedy antelopes are on the menu, including springbok, gazelles, and impalas.

SPEEDY FEATURES

✓ Long, thin legs
✓ Powerful muscles
✓ Long tail for balance
✓ Huge heart
✓ Stretchy spine

RUNNING SHOES

The cheetah's paws are different from those of other cats. The hard pads and non-retractable claws give extra grip at high speeds.

A cheetah can cover 22 ft (6.7 m) in a single stride!

Racehorses gallop at
43 mph (70 kph)

The world record for a race over two furlongs (0.25 miles/402 m) was 44 mph (70.8 kph). It was set in 2008.

BRED FOR SPEED

Thoroughbreds, quarterhorses, and other racehorses are slower over longer distances because they pace themselves. The record for a 1.5-mile (2.4-km) race is 38 mph (61 kph).

TYPICAL HORSE SPEEDS

Walk	2–5 mph (3.2–8 kph)	
Trot	7–10 mph (11.3–16 kph)	
Canter	10–17 mph (16–27.4 kph)	
Gallop	35–40 mph (56.3–64.4 kph)	

ICELANDIC HORSES HAVE SPECIAL MOVES

How a horse moves is called its gait. Most horses have four natural gaits— they can walk, trot, canter, or gallop.

Vikings took the first ponies to Iceland in the 800s CE.

MOVING TO THE BEAT

Every gait has its own beat, which comes from the rhythm of the horse's legs. Trotting is two-beat, because diagonal pairs of legs move together.

SPECIAL ICELANDIC GAITS

✓ **Tölt**
A four-beat gait that is faster than a walk, slower than a canter, and smoother than a trot.

✓ **Flying pace**
A two-beat gait of many small steps that's speedy and smooth over short distances.

THE GIBBON IS THE
KING OF THE SWINGERS

Out of all the primates, the gibbon is the best at swinging from branch to branch using only its arms.

Speed comes at a price! Most gibbons break a bone at least once in their life.

GREAT GIBBONS

Fast and agile, a gibbon can swing 50 ft (15 m) between branches at speeds up to 35 mph (56.3 kph). It has ball-and-socket wrist joints that rotate 360 degrees, long arms, long hands, and long, grasping fingers. The gibbon is also much smaller and lighter than any other ape.

SIFAKAS BOUND LIKE BALLERINAS

The sifaka is a kind of lemur. It spends most of its time in the trees.

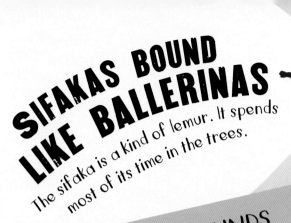

LEAPS AND BOUNDS

In the treetops, the sifaka doesn't swing. It crouches, runs, and leaps. It can jump as far as 33 ft (10 m) to a new tree. If the next tree is farther than that, the sifaka takes to the ground. It bounds along sideways on its back legs, using its front legs for balance.

Like all lemurs, sifakas live only in Madagascar.

Sadly, all nine sifaka species are endangered.

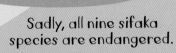

TOADS CRAWL AND FROGS JUMP

One of the ways to tell a toad from a frog is to look at how the animal moves.

toad

frog

Many frogs can jump more than 20 times their body length!

LOOKING AT LEGS

A toad's back legs are shorter than its head and body. It usually crawls along the ground, but it sometimes takes small hops. A frog has very long back legs with powerful muscles. It leaps high and long.

WONDROUS WEBBING

Frogs spend most of their lives in or near water. Many species have webbed back feet to help them swim. Most toads don't have webbed feet.

BADGERS DIG
THE FASTEST

American badgers can tunnel through the ground faster than any other animal.

Following food

A badger turns on its digging power when it is hunting. It targets rodents such as mice, gophers, and ground squirrels, but may also eat insects, snakes, birds, birds' eggs, reptiles or honey.

Badgers can run at 18.6 mph (30 kph)—that's more than twice as fast as an average man.

Shovel-like front paws with strong, curved claws allow the badger to dig forward or back. The animal's name comes from *bêcheur*, French for "digger."

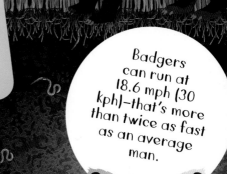

INSECTS WERE THE FIRST FLYERS

The first flying insects appeared 400 million years ago (mya), about 80 million years after the first land insects.

Meganeura

MONSTER DRAGONFLIES

The prehistoric dragonfly Meganeura's wings were more than 29.5 in (75 cm) across. It lived around 300 mya and fed on other insects, which it caught on the wing.

Not all insects can fly. Most ants can't.

Flower power

Wasps, bees, butterflies, beetles, and flies all evolved in the Cretaceous period (145–66 mya). They appeared at the same time as the first flowering plants.

fly

butterfly

wasp

bee

beetle

ARMY ANTS GO
ON THE MARCH

Ants live in groups called colonies.
Army ant colonies send out massive
raiding parties to find food.

rufous motmot

FEET FIRST FOR FOOD

A column of marching army ants can be 328 ft (100 m) long and over 3 ft (1 m) wide. As it surges forward, insects, spiders, worms, and other prey animals flee for their lives. The ants can catch up to 100,000 creatures a day.

The army ants are followed by rufous motmots and other birds. These "antbirds" pick off any creepy-crawlies stirred up by the ants.

ants carrying prey back to the colony

SWARMS AND FLOCKS

A big group of insects all moving together is a swarm; groups of birds are called flocks.

Ladybug swarms are most likely to appear before winter.

A murmuration of starlings can contain thousands of birds.

Starlings preparing to roost for the night swoop and dive acrobatically. Their display is called a murmuration.

medusa jellyfish

Thousands of krill swarm or "bloom" at the surface of the ocean.

krill, a small, shrimp-like crustacean

Global warming may be increasing the number of jellyfish swarms. Ouch!

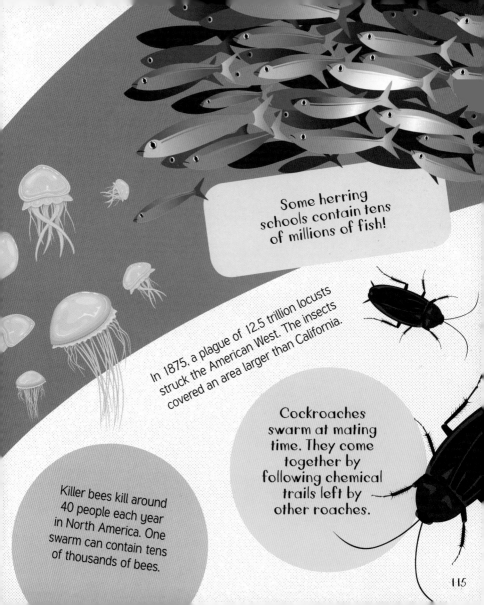

Some herring schools contain tens of millions of fish!

In 1875, a plague of 12.5 trillion locusts struck the American West. The insects covered an area larger than California.

Cockroaches swarm at mating time. They come together by following chemical trails left by other roaches.

Killer bees kill around 40 people each year in North America. One swarm can contain tens of thousands of bees.

MANTA RAYS
FLY UNDER WATER

Rays' closest relatives are sharks—but the two have completely different body shapes! Rays are flat and diamond-shaped, with winglike chest fins.

The pair of fins on a manta ray's head look like devil's horns!

FLAPPING FLIGHT

A ray swims by "flapping" its chest fins up and down. Each flap pushes water behind the fish and powers its body forward. If the ray keeps its mouth open, it can suck in plankton as it swims along.

Get outta here!

Mantas and other rays also "fly" OUT of the water! Mobula rays leap up to 6.6 ft (2 m) above the waves, staying airborne for two seconds or more.

BIRDS OF PREY

FLY WITHOUT TRYING

bald eagle

Birds of prey, or raptors, are heavy birds. Instead of using their own energy to stay airborne, they borrow energy FROM the air!

Harris's hawk

UPDRAFTS

As well as thermals, birds use updrafts— places where the wind is forced to blow upward because of an obstacle such as a mountainside, cliff, or large wave.

GLIDING SECRETS

Warm air rises. Birds of prey use currents of rising warm air called thermals to lift them high in the sky. The birds keep their wings outstretched, but they don't need to flap them!

SOME FISH
WALK ON LAND

Mudskippers live in muddy mangrove swamps and other shoreline habitats. Between the tides, when they are left out of the water, they "walk" around on their fins!

A mudskipper can breathe through its skin if it's wet, just like a frog.

AHOY
LANDLUBBERS

The mangrove rivulus can spend more than two months out of the water. It hides inside a fallen log. Like the mudskipper, it breathes through its skin!

The walking catfish of Southeast Asia can wiggle to a new pool or swamp if it has to.

mudskippers

SOME SNAKES SWIM IN THE SEA

All snakes can swim, but sea snakes actually live in the sea. They're usually found in tropical waters, around coral reefs.

MOVING METHOD

Snakes swim the same way that they travel across land. They move their bodies in an S-shape from side to side.

Just three drops of venom from a beaked sea snake is enough to kill eight people.

DEADLY VENOM

There are around 50 sea snake species. They all inject their prey with paralyzing venom. The black-banded sea krait's venom is ten times stronger than a cobra's.

black-banded sea krait

KANGAROOS ARE CHAMPION JUMPERS

Boing! Boing! Boing! All four kangaroo species share one energetic feature—their main way of moving around is hopping!

There are more kangaroos than humans in Australia.

TOP JUMPER

The red kangaroo is the largest, but it doesn't jump farthest or highest. That prize goes to the eastern grey kangaroo, which can cover 25 ft (7.6 m) in a single bound, and reach a height of 6 ft (1.8 m).

Kangaroos always move their back legs together when they hop, but they move them separately when they swim.

Kangaroos hang out in groups called "mobs." A mob can contain up to 100 kangaroos.

FLEAS LEAP MORE THAN
100 TIMES THEIR HEIGHT

Relative to their size, fleas are the best jumpers in the animal kingdom. No wonder they were once a star attraction at flea circuses!

HERE AND THERE

Fleas are parasites. Each kind specializes in a particular host, such as a cat, dog, or human. It sucks the host's blood for a while, then moves off. It might have to make as many as 10,000 jumps before it lands on a new host.

A flea jumps with the same amount of acceleration as a space rocket.

A flea can drink 15 times its own body weight in blood!

CROCODILES GALLOP

All the members of the crocodile family look similar, but some crocodiles have special moves.

THE HIGH WALK

Crocodiles and alligators usually walk low, with their legs bent out to the sides. However, smaller crocodile species can straighten up their legs for a "high walk" that pushes their body higher off the ground.

INTO A GALLOP

If a high-walking crocodile sees prey to pursue, it begins to bound and then gallop. First the front legs leap forward in sync, and then the back legs, picking up speed as they go.

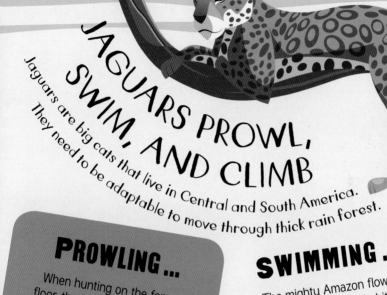

JAGUARS PROWL, SWIM, AND CLIMB

Jaguars are big cats that live in Central and South America. They need to be adaptable to move through thick rain forest.

PROWLING ...

When hunting on the forest floor, the jaguar slinks through the undergrowth. It carefully places one paw after the other, barely making a sound.

SWIMMING ...

The mighty Amazon flows through the jaguar's habitat. Taking to the river allows the cat to catch fish, turtles, and caimans (small crocodiles).

CLIMBING ...

Jaguars sometimes ambush their prey. They scale a tree and lie in wait until unsuspecting prey walk by.

123

Elephants, hippos, and
RHINOS CAN'T JUMP

These animals don't have flexible enough ankles to propel their bulk into the air.

CHARGE!

Rhinos can run faster than elephants. They charge at 34 mph (55 kph). Elephants only reach 25 mph (40 kph).

elephant

rhino

EXCEPTIONAL ELEPHANT

Like most animals, rhinos and hippos take all four feet off the ground when they run. Elephants don't do this.

hippo

GOATS LEAP OFF CLIFFS

Mountain goats are crazy climbers! They can keep their footing even when they're scaling sheer cliff faces.

Sometimes rival goats head-butt each other off cliff edges!

HIGHLAND FLING

If a goat gets stuck on a clifftop or remote ledge, there's only one solution—a giant leap! Goats have landed safely after leaping 39 ft (12 m) or more.

GRIPPING FEATURES

✓ Hooves' inner pads can push off from the ground.

✓ Cloven (split) hooves can spread apart.

✓ Each foot has a sharp dewclaw on its tip.

ANIMAL TRANSPORT

Horses may have been tamed for transport up to 6,500 years ago.

Some desert traders in North Africa and the Middle East still use camels as pack animals.

A mule is a cross between a donkey and a horse.

There are about 13,500 captive elephants in southern Asia.

Slow and steady, a donkey pulls heavy loads at 3.5 mph (5.6 kph).

Some Asian elephants work in the timber industry, hauling logs. Others transport tourists.

Two popular sports in the Middle East are camel racing and saluki dog racing.

The longest dog sled race is 1,049 miles (1,688 km). It takes teams at least 8 days to complete.

When Emperor Mansa Musa of Mali went to Makkah in the 1300s, a caravan of 80 camels carried his riches.

Water buffalo produce creamier milk than dairy cows. They can work the fields, too.

More people rely on water buffalo than on any other domesticated animal.

WARTHOGS RUN WITH THEIR TAIL UP

A warthog sticks up its tail as it trots along, so that the fluffy part points up at the sky.

SIMPLE SIGN

No one is sure why warthogs raise their tail when they run. Perhaps its upright position warns other warthogs of danger, so that they run, too! Warthogs live together in groups of up to 40 animals.

Warthogs have longer legs than other pigs. They can run at 34 mph (55 kph).

EMUS CAN'T
WALK BACKWARD

Emus are big, flightless birds, related to ostriches and cassowaries. Unlike ostriches, emus are unable to walk backward.

STAYING SAFE

Walking backward is a useful skill, especially when an animal is being threatened. No one knows why emus cannot do it. After all, they can't even fly from danger!

The emu is the only bird that has calf muscles.

FELLOW AUSSIE

Emus live in Australia, and so does another animal that can only go in one direction. All the traits that help the kangaroo take great forward bounds—its large feet, muscular legs, and big tail—also prevent it from going in reverse.

129

GIANT CLAMS STAY PUT

Some animals, including giant clams, reach a stage in their life when they won't travel anymore.

Adult barnacles never move, either!

YOUNG MOVERS

Giant clams have a very complicated life cycle. They hatch into tiny swimming trochophores and then become plankton—part of the ocean "soup" of larvae, other small creatures, and plants.

LIFE STAGES

Giant clams pass through several more life stages before they reach their adult form. Then they settle on the reef or seabed and never move again.

SLOW LORISES REALLY
ARE SLOW

The slow loris is a big-eyed primate that can spend hours not moving if threatened. It will remain motionless until the danger has passed.

Slow lorises are rare and small. The largest species weighs less than two bags of sugar. The smallest weighs just 14 oz (400 g).

WALKABOUT

Slow lorises live in Southeast Asia and are nocturnal hunters. They can cover a distance of 5 miles (8 km) in a night. They have an unusual way of moving, kind of like a snake.

The slow loris has a venomous bite!

GIANT TORTOISES
are the slowest reptiles

The giant Galapagos tortoise ambles along at just 0.16 mph (0.26 kph).

SLOW PACE

The Galapagos tortoise takes its time living, too—it doesn't reach maturity until age 25 and it can live to more than 150! Like all reptiles, the Galapagos tortoise cannot make its own body heat. It spends a couple of hours basking at the start of the day to warm up.

OTHER SLOWPOKES

The woodcock is the slowest bird. It flies along at just 5 mph (8 kph).

A garden snail can only travel 3.3 ft (1 m) per hour.

DINOSAURS COULD
outrun today's reptiles

bearded dragon

The fastest reptile around today is the bearded dragon, which dashes along at 25 mph (40 kph). The green iguana's next at 22 mph (35 kph).

DINOSAUR SPEEDSTERS

If they'd lived in dinosaur times, the bearded dragon and green iguana could have escaped a *T. rex*, which only moved at 12 mph (19 kph). But they couldn't have outrun *Ornithomimus* or *Gallimimus*. Those "ostrich mimics" bounded along at 45 mph (72 kph)!

Ornithomimus

SPEEDY HUNTER

Velociraptor means "speedy thief." This deadly predator could sprint at 40 mph (60 kph).

Gallimimus

The tiger beetle is the
FASTEST INSECT

The Australian tiger beetle runs at 4.2 mph (6.8 kph). That may not sound a lot, but it's the equivalent of 171 body lengths a second.

A cheetah travels 16 body lengths per second. Usain Bolt, the world's fastest man, covers six body lengths per second when he's sprinting.

Mite-y fast

The record for the fastest land animal relative to body length is held by another creepy-crawly. A mite from southern California has been recorded at a speed of 322 body lengths per second. Mites aren't insects. They are arachnids, part of the same group as spiders.

Ostriches are champion RUNNERS

The ostrich is the fastest bird on land. It runs at 43 mph (70 kph)—as fast as a greyhound!

BORN TO RUN

✓ Two toes per foot
✓ Large, hooflike toenails
✓ Powerful, long legs
✓ Killer kick

AFRICAN LIFE

Ostriches live in African savanna and desert. They share their habitat with lions, leopards, and cheetahs ... which is a good reason to run fast!

cassowary

The ostrich's closest relatives are rheas, emus, and cassowaries. The top speed for rheas is 40 mph (64 kph); for emus and cassowaries, it's 31 mph (50 kph).

Some lizards can RUN ON WATER

Meet the basilisk lizard! Its home is in Central America, where it lives in tropical rain forests.

ESCAPE ROUTE

The basilisk lizard spends most of its time in trees that overhang water. When threatened, it drops down and runs across the water's surface!

Pond skaters ...

... can also walk on water. They are so light that they can stand on its surface.

FANCY FEET

A basilisk lizard has long toes on its back feet. There are small folds on the edges of the toes. As the lizard runs, the folds open and trap pockets of air. The trapped air lets the lizard push against the water, instead of sinking.

GECKOS WALK
UPSIDE DOWN

The name gecko is meant to sound like the chirruping call it makes.

Geckos' feet can stick to any surface, no matter how smooth or slippery.

The smallest gecko is less than 0.8 in (2 cm) long.

The largest gecko was 23.5 in (60 cm) long.

HIDDEN HAIRS

Millions of microscopic hairs on its toe pads give the gecko its amazing grip. Each hair has hundreds of even more microscopic bristles. These hairs and bristles stick to surfaces like Velcro®.

There are nearly 1,000 species of gecko.

BRISTLES HELP WORMS TO WRIGGLE

A worm's body appears to have smooth segments. Seen through a microscope, however, it has groups of rough bristles on its underside.

WORM ENEMIES

Birds

Toads

Moles

Beetles

Snakes

Foxes

The world's biggest worm was found in South Africa. It was 22 ft (6.7 m) long!

MOVING STORY

The earthworm moves its bristles in and out to get a grip on the ground. It moves its segments forward or backward by stretching and contracting its muscles.

Snail slime is an ingredient in some face creams!

Slugs and snails
GLIDE ON SLIME

PEARLY PATH

Land slugs and snails move along on one large, muscular foot. This glides on a glittering trail of mucus produced by a gland just under the mouth. Slugs and snails belong to a special group of mollusks called gastropods, meaning "stomach foot."

MAGIC MUCUS

It's more than 95% water, but snail slime has some amazing properties. It sticks the snail to surfaces and stops its body from drying out.

A snail uses up nearly a third of its energy producing slime.

139

MINI MOVERS

A bumblebee beats its wings 200 times per second to stay airborne.

bumblebee

A butterfly's temperature must be around 85 °F (29.5 °C) for it to fly.

Adult cockroaches have wings, but they rarely use them. They prefer to scuttle!

peacock butterfly

A fly can move its two sets of wings independently.

house fly

The female winter moth's wings are too tiny for flight. Only the males can fly.

A headlouse can move 3.75 in (9.5 cm) per minute—the equivalent of the height of a giraffe in an hour!

A blowfly travels at 5.3 mph (8.6 kph). Horseflies are much faster, at 25 mph (40 kph).

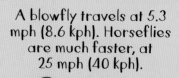

blowfly

A woodlouse has seven pairs of jointed legs. It's a crustacean, related to crabs and shrimps.

The silverfish is a wingless insect. As it wiggles along, it looks like a fish.

The hummingbird hawkmoth beats its wings 85 times per second—about 1.7 times faster than a hummingbird.

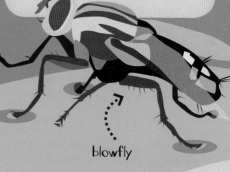

silverfish

SEA OTTERS GET TIED UP IN KNOTS

Sea otters live along the coasts of the northern Pacific Ocean. They have a neat trick for not floating away while they sleep.

SEAWEED STRAPS

Sea otters wrap strands of giant kelp around themselves. The seaweed is rooted to the seabed so it acts as an anchor for the sea otters.

SEAFOOD CRACKERS

When an otter is tethered to the kelp, it has both "hands" free! The clever sea mammal floats on its back and uses a stone as a simple tool to crack open shellfish and clams.

Penguins use wings AS FLIPPERS

Although they are birds, penguins are most at home swimming in the ocean. Over time their wings have evolved to be more like paddles or flippers.

macaroni penguin

Penguins' wings are stronger, relative to their size, than those of any other bird, but they aren't useful for flying. They are designed for swimming. Shaped like oars, they push the bird through the water.

Galapagos penguin

LIFE DOWN SOUTH

There are 17 penguin species. Apart from the Galapagos penguin, they all live in the Southern Hemisphere, or bottom half of the world.

CUTTLEFISH ARE
JET-POWERED

The cuttlefish is a relative of octopuses and squid. Most of the time it's a slow swimmer, but sometimes it puts on a burst of speed.

SWOOSHING WATER

When a cuttlefish spies a shark or other danger, it propels itself forward by rushing water through its mantle (the main part of its body). It also squirts out a cloud of ink to hide itself from the predator.

box jellyfish

oceanic whitetip shark

cuttlefish

A cuttlefish has blue-green blood and three hearts!

Jellyfish use very simple jet power, too.

Cuttlefish extend their tentacles to keep the body as streamlined as possible.

SCALLOPS SWIM BY SNAPPING THEIR SHELLS

Scallops don't move very fast or very far, but they can (sort of) "swim!"

The largest scallops are real whoppers. Their shells are 10 in (25.4 cm) across!

Shellfish with two hinged shells, like the scallop, are called bivalves.

CLAP! CLAP!

A scallop claps its shells by tensing and relaxing the muscle that connects them. The action forces water from the space between the shells and propels the scallop forward.

The scallop's shell is fringed by around 60 simple eyes. They can detect light and dark.

145

AMAZING MIGRATION

The Arctic tern flies at least 44,000 miles (71,000 km) a year, from the Arctic to the Antarctic and back again.

Desert locusts have migrated 2,795 miles (4,500 km) across the Atlantic.

Each year, 1.7 million wildebeest trek through Tanzania and Kenya. Their journey is called the Great Serengeti Migration.

Bar-tailed godwits make the longest single flight of any bird. They fly from Alaska to New Zealand.

Nearly half a million antelopes and 300,000 zebras also take part in the Great Serengeti Migration.

Bluefin tuna swim epic distances of up to 6,500 miles (10,500 km) to their spawning grounds.

Zooplankton migrate up and down. Swarms swim a vertical distance of 3,000 ft (915 m) every day.

In the wet season, 120 million red crabs migrate from the inland forests on Christmas Island. They travel to the coast to lay their eggs.

Each year, ten million fruit bats travel up to 1,250 miles (2,000 km) to different feeding grounds in Zambia.

Spiny lobsters march along the seabed to deeper waters each winter—a distance of up to 30 miles (50 km) each way.

Elephant seals make two 13,050-mile (21,000-km) migrations every year.

HUMPBACK WHALES MIGRATE FROM THE POLES TO THE TROPICS

The humpback travels at least 5,250 miles (8,500 km) from polar waters to the tropics and back again every year.

NORTH AND SOUTH

Humpback populations stick to their half of the world and don't cross the equator!

Northern humpbacks have summer from June to September.

Southern humpbacks have summer from December to March.

THE WHALE'S YEAR

Humpbacks spend summer feasting on krill, fish, or squid in polar waters. They put on up to 10 tons (9 tonnes) of blubber! They head to warmer waters to mate and give birth.

Caribou make the longest
MIGRATION ON FOOT

Some caribou make two 600-mile (965.6-km) treks every year. They spend their lives on the move.

Summer sedge

In summer, a lush green plant called cotton grass carpets the Arctic's treeless tundra. Caribou arrive in May, have their calves here, and stay till July. Then they head south to spend winter in sheltered boreal forests.

TUNDRA DANGERS

Arctic wolves

Mosquitoes and other biting insects

Polar bears

There are about 750,000 wild caribou in Alaska.

European and Russian caribou are known as reindeer.

Monarch butterflies MAKE RECORD-BREAKING JOURNEYS

These beautiful butterflies have come up with a plan for surviving cold winters.

The monarch's orange-and-black wings warn predators that it's toxic!

STANDARD LIFE CYCLE

A monarch caterpillar hatches, munches leaves, forms a chrysalis, and emerges as a butterfly—all in fewer than 40 days. Usually, it reproduces and dies, but ...

... monarchs that emerge at the end of summer don't mate. Instead, they feast and fly south. They spend winter in the pine forests of California and Mexico. In spring, they head north, and only THEN do they mate!

LEATHERBACKS
SWIM EPIC DISTANCES

One tagged turtle swam an extraordinary 12,774 miles (20,558 km) across the Pacific in 647 days.

PACIFIC AND ATLANTIC

Leatherbacks live in the Pacific and Atlantic oceans. Pacific ones spend summer stuffing themselves with jellyfish off the coast of California. Their nesting beaches are in Southeast Asia. Atlantic leatherbacks feed off the east coast of Canada and nest in the Caribbean.

BIG BEASTS

Leatherbacks are the largest sea turtles. They can weigh up to 2,000 lb (900 kg)—that's as much as a cow—and they are longer than a kingsize bed.

SALMON DON'T REALLY RUN IN A SALMON RUN

The salmon "run" is the journey that salmon make from the ocean then upriver to their spawning grounds.

A FISH'S LIFE

Salmon spend their early life in rivers, but as adults they swim out to sea. They fatten up in the ocean. After a few years, they are fully grown. They return to the rivers to spawn (lay their eggs).

RIVER RUN

Swimming against the current of a river is tough, but salmon are strong and muscular. In places, they have to leap up mini waterfalls. The fish that survive the journey spawn and then die, completely exhausted.

EELS MAKE JOURNEYS OF
2,730 miles (6,000 km)

The European eel's mammoth migration
even takes it slithering across land!

COMING AND GOING

Eels begin life as plankton-like larvae
in the open ocean, leave it as pencil-
sized young elvers, then return
years later as adults. In between,
they live in rivers and streams.
Their leathery, slime-coated
skin allows them to cross
land to find new habitats.

MATURE EELS

Male eels spend up to 12 years
in fresh water, and females up
to 20. Then they make the long
journey back to the ocean to
breed. Their dark bodies
turn silver for better
camouflage in the
open ocean.

SHARKS HAVE AN
EXTRA EYELID

A protective lid covers a shark's eyes when it attacks—in most species, anyway!

mako shark

A VIEW THROUGH

The third eyelid is see-through, so the shark can still see when it is shut. It slides across the eye from under the bottom eyelid.

SPECIAL CASE

The great white shark doesn't have a third eyelid. When it's feeding, it rolls its pupil back in its head to avoid any damage from thrashing prey.

great white shark

eagle

ANIMALS WITH THIRD EYELIDS

Frogs

Crocodiles

Sea Lions

Camels

Birds

Cats

150

SNAKES DON'T HAVE EYELIDS

These slithering reptiles wear glasses instead!

Snakes can't blink. They sleep with their eyes open.

SINGLE SCALE

Rather than having movable eyelids, a snake has one clear scale over each eye. The scale protects the eye from damage or drying out.

GOODBYE, HELLO!

A snake loses its eye scales when it sheds its skin—there are new ones waiting underneath. Just before shedding, the eye scale turns cloudy.

Fish don't have eyelids, either.

DRAGONFLY EYES HAVE
THOUSANDS OF LENSES

Up to 30,000 light sensors help dragonflies build up a mosaic-like picture of the world.

Eyes with many lenses are called compound eyes. Many insects have them, and dragonflies and bees have the most lenses of all. Their huge eyes wrap around the head like a motorcycle helmet, giving nearly 360 degree sight!

RAINBOW VISION

Three different light-sensing proteins in our eyes mean we see in combinations of red, blue, and green. But some dragonflies detect up to 30 different pigments, including UV!

Dragonflies that hunt at dusk don't have as many pigment receptors as ones that are active in the day.

SOME ANIMALS SEE IN BLACK AND WHITE

Animals that have only one type of light-sensing cone in their eyes can only see in shades of white and black.

owl monkey

NIGHT SIGHT, LOW LIGHT

For animals that are active at night or that live in low light, seeing shape and movement is more important than shades.

walrus

TWO-TONE

Owl monkeys and raccoons are just two nocturnal creatures that are monochromatic (only able to see in black and white). In the ocean, sharks, skates, seals, sea lions, and walruses live in these shades, too.

SNAKES DETECT INFRARED

The infrared (IR) spectrum is invisible to humans, but not to snakes.

USING HEAT

Rattlesnakes, boas, pit vipers, and other snakes can "see" body heat coming off their victims. They don't detect IR with their eyes, but with sensors between their eyes and nostrils. This super sense allows them to strike with deadly accuracy.

HEAT TRACKERS

Snakes even detect body heat lingering in animals' tracks. It's as if they have built-in night-vision goggles or a thermal camera!

IR DETECTORS

✓ Mosquito
✓ Piranha
✓ Goldfish

SOME ANIMALS SEE ULTRAVIOLET

Ultraviolet (UV) is another kind of light that humans can't see, but some animals can.

SECRET MESSAGES

Many flowers need insects to visit them to pick up pollen and carry it to other flowers. Some have UV markings that are only visible to bees and butterflies. These markings guide the insects in like landing-strip lights!

human view
(no UV sensitivity)

bee view
(UV sensitivity)

HIDDEN SIGNS

Some birds and butterflies have patterns on their feathers or wing scales that are only visible in UV. We can't see them, but their mates can!

159

A SNAIL'S EYES ARE ON STRETCHY STALKS

Land snails have eyes at the end of their tentacles.

eye

When a snail detects danger, it hides in its shell, with its tentacles tucked in.

SENSATIONAL TENTACLES

Land snails have two pairs of tentacles. The longest ones, also called eyestalks, have eyes at the tips. The shorter pair carries organs for detecting smell. The more a snail waves its tentacles around, the more it sees and smells.

smell organ

MAGICAL MYSTERY

Most water snails' eyes are at the base of their tentacles, but the mystery snail's are at the tip like a land snail's. If a predator bites off its eyestalk, the mystery snail can regrow its eye!

CAVE FISH SEE WITH
THEIR MOUTHS

Fish in cave habitats have lost the power of sight,
but they can still determine distance.

USE IT OR LOSE IT

In their dark home, cave fish don't need
to see, and over millions of years they've
stopped being able to. They navigate by
producing bursts of suction with their
mouths. This creates pressure waves that
the fish use to measure the distance
of objects

cave fish

BLIND CAVE ANIMALS

✓ Spiders

✓ Crabs

✓ Salamanders

✓ Beetles

cave crab

The blind
cave crab
lives in caves on
the Indonesian
island of
Sulawesi.

MOLES ARE NEARLY BLIND... AND SO ARE MOLE-RATS

Moles have teeny-tiny eyes that can tell the difference between light and dark, but not much else.

DOWN BELOW

A mole spends its life underground. It uses its outsize front feet to scoop out tunnels. Other senses—touch, smell, and hearing—make up for the mole's lack of sight.

HAIRLESS RODENTS

Naked mole-rats aren't moles or rats. They're close relatives of guinea pigs. Like moles, they are nearly blind. They live in underground colonies of 20 to 300 animals.

mole

naked mole-rat

Earthworms don't have
EARS OR EYES

A worm's most important sense is touch.

There are about 6,000 different species of earthworm.

SENSORY SKIN

An earthworm's body is covered in nerve endings and sense organs. The nerve endings are for touch. They detect different textures in the worm's surroundings and pick up vibrations. The sense organs "smell" and "taste."

IN THE DARK

An earthworm may not have eyes, but it can still sense light. It needs to avoid sunlight, which can dry out its skin.

163

INSECT SENSES

A male luna moth's feathery feelers can sniff out a female 6.5 miles (11 km) away.

Unlike adult butterflies, caterpillars can hardly see. Their simple eyes sense only light and dark.

Tiger moths can not only hear bats' sonar—they can jam it! The moths confuse the bats by creating fake echoes.

Wasps have an amazing sense of smell. They can even be trained to sniff out explosives and drugs.

praying mantis

The praying mantis's main sense is sight. It has two large eyes and three simple eyes located between them.

wasp or yellow jacket

A fly has sensory hairs all over its feet. It can taste something by walking on it!

Fire beetles flock to forest fires to lay their eggs in burned wood. Infrared sensors under the beetles' legs show them the way.

The cockchafer beetle can fan out the end of its feelers. This helps it to sense sounds and smells, and find food.

cricket

A cricket's ears are tiny—and they're not where you'd expect. They are just under the insect's knees.

Ants have about 400 smell and taste receptors—more than any other insect. Fruit flies have 61.

SOME SHARKS HAVE HAMMER-SHAPED HEADS

The hammerhead shark is one of the oddest-looking sharks.

THE EYES HAVE IT

A hammerhead's eyes are on the sides of its head, so it can see all around. It has better binocular vision than sharks with closer-set eyes.

The hammerhead swings its head from side to side as it swims.

FAVE FOODS

- ✓ Stingrays
- ✓ Other sharks
- ✓ Other fish
- ✓ Octopuses
- ✓ Squid
- ✓ Crustaceans

The smallest hammerhead is just 2.3 ft (70 cm) long. The largest is a whopping 20 ft (6 m).

OWLS HAVE ALL-AROUND VISION

Owls have enormous, forward-facing eyes that sit in bony eye sockets.

LOOKING AROUND

An owl cannot move or swivel its eyes, but it still has good all-around vision. That's because it can turn its head up to 270 degrees left or right and almost upside down!

BINOCULARS!

Forward-facing eyes give an owl good binocular vision (seeing an object with both eyes at the same time). That means it can see in three dimensions (height, width, and depth) and also judge distance.

COLOSSAL SQUID HAVE THE BIGGEST EYES

They are also the biggest invertebrates in the animal kingdom!

WHAT A PLATEFUL!

Each of the colossal squid's eyes is 12 in (30 cm) across—the size of a dinner plate! But very few of these creatures have ever been seen. Some individuals might have even bigger peepers!

The colossal squid grows to 50 ft (15 m) or more. It hunts in deep waters around Antarctica. Its slightly smaller cousin, the giant squid, has eyes that are 10 in (25.4 cm)—about the size of a basketball.

WATCH OUT!

Sperm whales hunt colossal and giant squid.

sperm whale

TARSIERS HAVE THE LARGEST EYES OF ANY MAMMAL...

...relative to their size, at least!

EVERYTHING IS RELATIVE

Each eye is only about 0.6 in (16 mm) across, but a tarsier's whole body is only about the same size as a squirrel!

NIGHT VISION

Big eyes let in maximum light, and the tarsier certainly needs it. This little primate is a night hunter in the rain forests of Southeast Asia. It catches insects, small birds, bats, lizards, and snakes.

Each of the tarsier's eyes weighs more than its brain!

169

CATS HAVE MIRRORS IN THEIR EYES

Like many night hunters, cats have a special way of seeing in the dark.

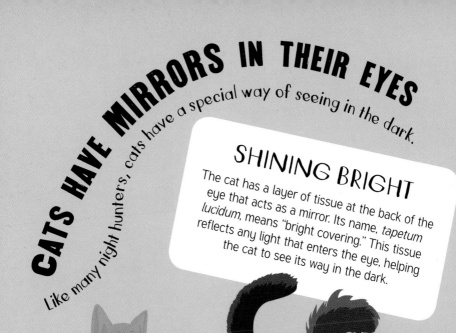

SHINING BRIGHT

The cat has a layer of tissue at the back of the eye that acts as a mirror. Its name, *tapetum lucidum*, means "bright covering." This tissue reflects any light that enters the eye, helping the cat to see its way in the dark.

CAUGHT ON CAMERA

Take a picture of a cat and you'll probably see its *tapetum lucidum*. In the photograph, the eyes reflect the camera flash and seem to shine.

MOST SPIDERS HAVE EIGHT EYES

About 99 percent of spider species have four pairs of eyes.

HEY, BIG EYES!

Daytime hunters, such as jumping spiders, have better eyesight than ones that are active at night. Their larger, forward-facing eyes pick out details and even different shades!

PREY DETECTORS

Usually positioned on the sides of the head, the spider's other eyes are just simple sensors. They detect light, dark, and movement.

Some spiders have no eyes. Others have as many as six pairs!

SOME MOLES HAVE STAR-SHAPED NOSES

Star-nosed moles have the strangest noses.

SUPERSTARS

Star-nosed moles live underground and are almost completely blind. But their nose makes up for their lack of eyesight. It's surrounded by 22 super-sensitive tentacles that stick out like the points of a star.

TELLING SMELLS

The star-nosed mole's tentacles help it to sniff out insects, worms, and other invertebrates. It can even smell underwater! The mole is a strong swimmer and catches fish and crayfish.

172

A KIWI HAS AN AMAZING SENSE OF SMELL

This flightless New Zealand bird sniffs out earthworms and small crustaceans.

SNIFF AND SNORT

The kiwi lives in rough grassland but also hunts along the shoreline. It prods its long beak into the leaf litter or sand. Its nostrils are at the end of this beak, so the bird has to snort out air to stop them from clogging up!

The kiwi nests on the ground because it cannot fly.

Relative to its size, only one bird has a larger olfactory bulb (smell organ) than the kiwi—the condor!

173

GREAT WHITES SMELL BLOOD
FROM 3 MILES (5 KM) AWAY

No shark is more feared than the great white—with good reason!

A great white can detect one drop of blood in one million drops of water.

Two-thirds of the great white's brain is for processing smell.

As well as being able to see, hear, feel, smell, and taste, sharks detect electrical signals.

HOW SHARKS SMELL

Seawater washes smells into the great white's nostrils. If the shark smells prey—especially an animal that is already injured and weak—it heads toward it.

Sharks use their sense of smell to find a mate and to navigate, too.

ELEPHANT TRUNKS DO MORE THAN SMELL

Two nostrils run up the length of an elephant's trunk, but this structure is not simply a nose!

TRUNK TRICKS

- ✓ Smelling
- ✓ Breathing
- ✓ Grasping objects
- ✓ Squirting water
- ✓ Feeding
- ✓ Lifting weights
- ✓ DIY snorkel
- ✓ Sensing thunder
- ✓ Stroking
- ✓ Slapping

SMELL STORY

Elephants are even more sensitive to smells than bloodhounds. They have millions of receptor cells inside their trunks. Around 2,000 of their genes are dedicated to smelling, compared to fewer than 400 of yours.

UNUSUAL SENSES

Some animals can tell when a storm's on the way—especially prey animals, such as wild sheep and goats.

Most lizards have a "third eye" on the top of their head that is sensitive to light.

A jerboa's huge ears give it keen hearing. They also release body heat and keep it cool.

Bats use a form of sonar. They squeak then see how long the echoes take to come back. It tells them what's near.

Dogs seem to detect cancer and other medical conditions. They can smell chemical changes in their owners.

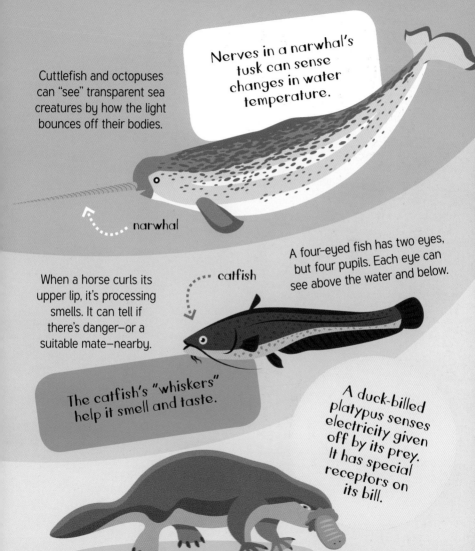

Cuttlefish and octopuses can "see" transparent sea creatures by how the light bounces off their bodies.

Nerves in a narwhal's tusk can sense changes in water temperature.

narwhal

When a horse curls its upper lip, it's processing smells. It can tell if there's danger—or a suitable mate—nearby.

catfish

A four-eyed fish has two eyes, but four pupils. Each eye can see above the water and below.

The catfish's "whiskers" help it smell and taste.

A duck-billed platypus senses electricity given off by its prey. It has special receptors on its bill.

177

SEA COWS HAVE WHISKERS ALL OVER

Manatees and dugongs are covered in touch-sensitive hairs.

TACTILE HAIRS

A manatee has about 2,000 of these touch-sensitive hairs on its face, and 3,000 more on the rest of its body. They are connected to nerve fibers and sensory receptors that send messages back to the brain.

TOUCH AND FEEL

The manatee's face hairs touch and grasp sea grass, algae, and other food. The body hairs pick up information that tells them where they are in the water.

Seals have the most
SENSITIVE WHISKERS

Seals, sea lions, and walruses use their whiskers to track down prey in murky water.

The seal has muscles to move its whiskers for a better "feel."

MOVEMENT TRACES

When a fish swims, it disturbs the water. It leaves behind a wake, or movement trails.

WHISKERS AND WAKES

Seals' whiskers are sensitive enough to detect a wake from at least 600 ft (180 m) away. They can even picture the size and shape of the fish that left it!

179

BEES TALK
by dancing!

It's the job of worker bees to fly around looking for new food sources. When a bee finds a good patch of flowers, it flies back to the hive to tell the other bees.

THE WAGGLE DANCE

1 The bee walks in a wiggly line. The angle of the line shows where food is, compared to the sun.

2 The bee then circles back to the bottom of its original line . . .

3 . . . and draws the straight line again. The longer the bee waggles for, the farther away the food source is.

4 The bee circles the other way back to the bottom and starts again.

180

TREE FROGS BEAT WITH THEIR FEET

Some tree frogs use vibrations–shakings of the air–to communicate in the noisy rain forest.

SHAKE IT!

The red-eyed tree frog sends out vibrations to warn other frogs off its territory. It creates them by shaking branches with its back legs. It sends out vibrations when it wants to attract a mate, too.

BABY BOOMERS

Tree frogs can "read" vibrations even before they are born. If they sense a snake coming near, the tadpoles hatch from their eggs early and drop to safety.

181

THE GRASSHOPPER MOUSE HOWLS LIKE A WOLF

This tiny rodent is a fierce—and noisy—hunter.

SOLO ARTIST

The grasshopper mouse stands on its back legs and howls at the sky. It is laying claim to its territory—just like a songbird when it sings, but not nearly so sweet!

HOWLING WOLF

The grasshopper mouse's squeaks are outside the range of human hearing. However, played back at a slower speed, they sound just like a wolf's howls!

Mice communicate with each other by leaving scent trails, too.

182

WOLVES REALLY DO
HOWL AT THE MOON

Howling is how wolves communicate with each other.

A wolf's howl can be heard up to 10 miles (16 km) away.

Packs of wolves sometimes howl together as a chorus.

HOW TO HOWL

Wolves are most active at night, so that's when they need to communicate. They point their face up when they howl to make the sound carry farther. They look as if they are howling at the sky.

Different wolf species have their own "accents," or dialects.

WHALE MUSIC IS CONSTANTLY CHANGING

Humpback whales are famous for their amazing songs.

MUSIC EVOLUTION

Male humpbacks sing, not females. Strangely, all the males in one area sing the same song. The song slowly changes, sometimes borrowing from songs they hear from other groups.

Humpbacks sing at 30–8,000 Hz.

Humans talk at 85–255 Hz.

LONG-DISTANCE LOWS

The lowest sounds that the whale makes can travel more than 10,000 miles (16,000 km) through the water.

DOLPHINS CLICK AND WHISTLE

These clever sea mammals communicate by whistling.

Clicking the way

Dolphins' clicks aren't for communicating. Listening to how clicks bounce off surrounding objects helps the animals to navigate. It's called echolocation.

SIGNATURE WHISTLES

Dolphins recognize each other by the sounds they make. Every dolphin has its own unique whistle.

Dolphins also communicate by touch and body language.

A WHISTLE CAN MEAN...

✓ "There's lots of fish over here!"

✓ "Shark nearby—watch out!"

✓ "Mom, I'm lost!"

✓ AND MORE...

FIREFLIES USE LIGHTS TO SEND MESSAGES

Fireflies are beetles that can light up.

LIGHT DISPLAY

Adult fireflies flash their lights on and off in a pattern. It's their way of saying that they are looking for a mate. Big groups can create quite a display on a summer evening!

There are more than 2,000 firefly species.

GLOWING GRUBS

Firefly larvae can produce light, too. They glow to warn predators that they don't taste good, so it's best to leave them alone.

"BIOLUMINESCENCE" means light produced by a living organism.

SOME FROGS BELLOW LIKE BULLS

The bullfrog gets its name from the loud sounds it makes.

FROG CHORUS

In early summer, bullfrog males become super-noisy. It's breeding season! They bellow to attract females and frighten off other males. Spaced evenly around a pond or lake, each bullfrog hopes females like his song best.

LITTLE MIX

At 90 decibels, the bullfrog's call is noisier than a lawnmower. Amazingly, a tree frog called the coqui is just as loud, though it's only one-quarter the size of a bullfrog!

One bullfrog weighs as much as four hamsters.

SCARING OFF PREDATORS

The harmless milk snake is disguised to look like the deadly coral snake. Both are red, black, and yellow.

The lionfish is named for its frilly "mane." It helps the fish look bigger than it really is.

The horned lizard has a repulsive way to discourage predators. It fires blood at them from its eyes!

The rough-skinned newt has an orange belly—a warning for predators that it contains poisons.

The sea slug has stinging cells to protect itself. The bright skin warns would-be hunters.

pink butterfly fish

The hoatzin's other name is the "stink bird." It deters predators by smelling like cow dung.

Many animals have eye spots–huge spots that could be mistaken for eyes belonging to a much larger creature.

A tiny bird called the brown thornbill can mimic the call of a hawk. It does this to scare predators away from its nest.

The bombardier beetle sprays explosive chemicals at any attacker. BOOM!

A skunk scares off bears or other predators by squirting a foul, stinky liquid from its anus!

189

OCTOPUSES BLUSH

An octopus can turn pinky-red, but it doesn't mean it's embarrassed.

SKIN STORY

1 The skin can reveal the octopus's mood. Red means annoyed!

2 The octopus can change its appearance to blend in with the background.

3 The octopus can darken different parts of its body to make itself look scarier!

HIDE AND SEEK

An octopus has no bones and is super-flexible. It can squeeze into the tiniest crack or crevice if it needs to hide from a predator.

HOVERFLIES PRETEND TO BE WASPS

They have yellow-and-black markings, just like wasps or hornets.

wasp

HIGH-VIS JACKETS

Wasps and hornets wear yellow and black as a warning sign. It tells other insects that they carry a painful sting, so it is best to steer clear.

hoverfly

IN DISGUISE

Hoverflies are black and yellow, too, even though they aren't dangerous. Being disguised to look like wasps means that they're not eaten by birds or other predators—they move along in case they get stung!

FRILLED LIZARDS PUFF OUT THEIR NECKS

It's a trick to make the lizard look bigger!

Frilled lizards are up to 3 ft (90 cm) long.

FEARSOME FRILL

The frilled lizard has a pleated flap of skin around its neck. If it feels threatened, it unfurls its neck frill and hisses. If this display doesn't terrify the attacker, the little lizard races up the nearest tree.

Frilled lizards hatch from their eggs as miniature adults, complete with a working frill!

GROUNDED

Frilled lizards live mostly in the trees, except when they're tempted down to catch small lizards, rodents, or other prey.

PUFFERFISH BLOW UP LIKE BALLOONS

These strange little fish are some of the weirdest creatures in the ocean!

PRICKLY BUSINESS

There are around 190 puffer fish species. None are a typical fish shape—some even look like little cubes or pyramids. When threatened, they puff up to show off their prickly spines.

RISKY FOOD

Pufferfish contain deadly toxins. Strangely, their meat is a delicacy in some parts of the world. Trained chefs remove most of the toxins, leaving just enough to give the diner a tingly tongue!

MOSQUITOES HUM
TO ATTRACT A MATE

Whatever you might think, the buzz of the mosquito isn't just a warning that YOU are about to be bitten!

BEATING BUZZ

The buzzy hum comes from the mosquito's moving wings, which beat up to 600 times per second. When a male and female meet, their wings rise and fall in time and produce the same hum! How romantic!

DEADLY KILLER

Male mosquitoes feed on nectar, but females need to suck blood to nourish their eggs. Their bites can be deadly.

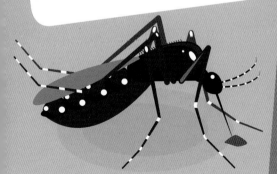

MOSQUITO-CARRIED DISEASES

✓ Malaria

✓ Yellow fever

✓ Dengue fever

✓ Encephalitis

BOWERBIRDS
COLLECT GARBAGE

Bowerbirds can't sing or dance— but they're amazing artists!

BEAUTIFYING THE BOWER

1 Build a structure called a bower from sticks and grass.

2 Carpet the display area in front of the bower with moss.

3 Arrange piles of bright objects. Group all the reds together, all the blues, and so on...

ART OBJECTS

✓ Flowers

✓ Fruits

✓ Beetle shells

✓ Broken glass or ceramics

✓ Plastic toys

195

DAZZLING
DISPLAYS

Male guppy fish dance and swish their tails to attract a mate.

Male peacocks start to grow their fancy tail feathers at the age of two.

The male peacock spider displays the flashy markings on its abdomen to a female—just like a feathered peacock shows off its blue-and-green tail!

Some male spiders court females with a silk-wrapped gift of food.

Red-crowned crane couples perform complicated courtship dances.

196

Bright feathers aren't enough for the male bird-of-paradise—it puts on an acrobatic display, too!

The male frigate bird has a huge, bright-red, inflatable throat sac. When it's puffed out, the females certainly notice him!

The male hooded seal has a pink "nose balloon." He attracts attention from females by inflating it.

Stags roar to impress females. They may drag their antlers through a bush, too. If they snag some vegetation, it'll make them look bigger!

Male hippos and porcupines are just two of the animals that court a female by peeing on her.

CAPUCHIN MONKEYS TELL LIES

These fresh monkeys sometimes give false alarms!

STANDING IN LINE

When a troop of capuchins finds a source of bananas or other yummy food, the highest-ranking ones eat their fill first.

LIES AND LUNGES

The monkeys waiting their turn sometimes use a little deception. They make a hiccupping noise that means a predator is near. It scares away the high-ranking monkeys long enough for the tricksters to dart in and grab some food!

Capuchins are named after French monks who wore cloaks with brown hoods.

HOWLERS ARE THE LOUDEST MONKEYS

This monkey's howl can be heard through thick forest from 3 miles (5 km) away!

TALKING TERRITORY

Howler monkeys are South America's biggest monkeys. They live in troops of up to 20. Each troop has its territory, and the males howl to defend it.

RECORD BREAKER

Howler monkeys are especially noisy at the start and end of the day. Their calls can reach 128 decibels, making them the loudest land animal.

A howler monkey's tail is about as long as its head and body together—up to 36 in (92 cm)!

MOCKINGBIRDS
ARE MIMICS

The clue to the mockingbird's trick is in its name. It "mocks" another animal's call!

COVER VERSIONS

The male mockingbird can copy other birds' songs. To human ears, his songs sound like exact copies, but female mockingbirds can tell the difference.

A mockingbird can learn 150 songs or more.

Mockingbirds also mimic noises made by frogs, dogs, and car alarms!

IMPRESSIVE!

Females choose the males that sing the most songs. Maybe it's a way of guaranteeing a mature mate—after all, it takes time to learn all those calls.

KAKAPOS ARE SUPER-LOUD

Kakapos are the noisiest parrots.

CALLING ALL FEMALES!

The male kakapo's low, booming call to attract a mate can travel as far as 3.1 miles (5 km). To amplify the sound and bounce it farther, the male digs out a little bowl-shaped stage and stands in the middle of it!

CRITICALLY ENDANGERED

The kakapo lives in New Zealand. It had no natural predators there, so it lost the ability to fly. Later, it was easy prey for dogs and other transplanted animals. Today there are fewer than 160 kakapos left in the wild.

KOOKABURRAS LAUGH

There is a famous song about the kookaburra's laugh.

CACKLING CALL

The kookaburra makes a long, hooting cackle at dawn and dusk. Like many bird calls, this one tells other birds about its territory. Shorter laughs warn of danger or let other family members know where they are.

QUICK RESPONSE

If a kookaburra hears another kookaburra laughing nearby, it will laugh back—even if the laugh is just a recording.

WALRUSES WHISTLE

Walruses also bark, grunt, bellow, growl, rasp, and click!

MAKE SOME NOISE

For everyday communication, walruses bark—just like their close relatives, seals and sea lions. But at breeding time, bulls (males) show off many more calls. Most are produced by the vocal cords, but there are also spooky, bell-like sounds from inflatable air sacs in the throat.

Tusky talk

Male walruses communicate with their tusks. They show off their length—up to 3 ft (90 cm)—and bash rivals with them!

Walruses are HUGE! They can weigh up to 1.5 tons (1.4 tonnes)!

ORCAS ARE
SCARIER THAN SHARKS

Orcas (also called killer whales) and sharks are the ocean's apex predators.

An orca's brain weighs nearly 200 times more than a great white's.

TOP HUNTERS

Apex predators are right at the top of the food chain, with no other animal hunting them. Sharks have a fierce reputation, but at least most species work alone—orcas hunt in groups like wolf packs!

All ashore

Some clever killer whales deliberately "beach" themselves to catch seal pups. They know that the next wave will carry them back out to sea.

204

BEARS ARE THE BIGGEST
LAND PREDATORS

Polar bears and Alaskan brown bears are huge hunters.

brown bear

FILLING UP

Bears will eat anything! Brown bears are famous for catching salmon in early summer. Polar bears hunt seals, birds, and fish. Both bears hunt mammals too, from rodents to reindeer.

EATING GREENS

Meat is only a small part of a brown bear's diet. Mostly it feeds on grass, fruit, insects, nuts, roots, and leaves. Polar bears sometimes eat kelp or berries.

polar bear

ringed seal

BLACK MAMBAS HAVE A DEADLY BITE

These venomous snakes are also very fast movers!

A bite from a black mamba can kill a person in twenty minutes.

DEADLY SPEEDSTER

Over short distances, a black mamba can probably hit speeds of 12.5 mph (20 kph). Once it catches its prey, it delivers a paralyzing bite. Then it waits for the poison to take effect.

ON THE MENU

Black mambas hunt bats, chickens, bushbabies (a kind of primate), and other snakes. They live in grasslands and forests in sub-Saharan Africa.

GABOON VIPERS
HAVE THE LONGEST FANGS

Gaboon vipers also pump out more venom than any other snake.

FANG ATTACK

A gaboon viper's fangs are 2 in (5 cm) long. Once they pierce a victim's flesh, they can inject a couple of teaspoonfuls of venom. The snake is an ambush killer. It lies hidden on the forest floor and then strikes a passing bird or mammal.

HEAVY!

Gaboon vipers can grow to 6 ft (1.8 m) long and weigh more than 45 lb (20 kg). They are Africa's heaviest venomous snake.

THE BIGGEST
SEA SNAIL FEEDS ON WORMS

This beastly mollusk hunts strange, bristly marine worms.

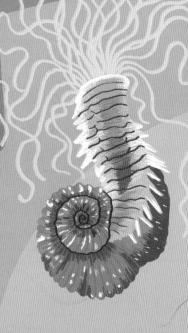

OUT TO DINNER

Known as the giant whelk or Australian trumpet, the huge snail lives in waters off northern Australia and Southeast Asia. It waves a special sense organ to sniff out the worms, and has sharp, rasping teeth for ripping through their flesh.

Whopping whelk

The giant whelk weighs up to 40 lb (18 kg). Its shell, which can be 3 ft (91 cm) long, is popular with collectors.

JELLYFISH
LASSO THEIR PREY

Long tentacles help the jellyfish to catch a meal.

CATCHING PREY

Stinging cells along the jellyfish's trailing tentacles snag on plankton, crustaceans, and small fish. The stingers have barbs that inject poison and paralyze the prey.

STING STEALER

Sea slugs prey on jellyfish and steal their stings. First, the slug slimes all over the jellyfish so it cannot fire defensive stinging cells. Then, when the slug eats the jellyfish, the stingers pass to pouches on its body. The slug can fire them out if it comes under attack!

SOME SNAKES HUG PREY TO DEATH

Not all snakes kill with venom—some wrap around their prey instead.

African rock python

POWERFUL PRESSURE

Snakes that squeeze are called constrictors. They include boas and pythons. These are the largest snakes in the world, so they have plenty of crushing power.

TOP 5 CONSTRICTORS

Green anaconda	550 lb (249 kg)
Reticulated python	350 lb (160 kg)
African rock python	250 lb (113 kg)
Burmese python	200 lb (91 kg)
Indian python	200 lb (91 kg)

green anaconda

DRAGONS
HAVE DEADLY BITES

The reptile with the deadliest bite is the Komodo dragon.

LARGE LIZARD

About the same length as a tiger, the Komodo dragon is the largest lizard. It's named after one of the Indonesian islands where it lives.

KILLER KOMODO

Mostly, the Komodo dragon eats carrion. But it also kills large prey, including water buffalo, deer, pigs, monkeys, and even humans. Its jaws aren't very powerful, but it has a venomous bite and sharp, knifelike teeth.

Komodo dragons are cannibals. Younger Komodos make up a tenth of their diet!

211

AMBUSH
PREDATORS

The trapdoor spider's burrow has a hinged trapdoor. The spider bursts out to catch insects, frogs, and mice.

The yellow-tailed scorpion strikes woodlice by the entrance to its lair.

The common snapping turtle "hunts" by staying very still. If prey comes close, the turtle's head darts forward to snap it up.

Crab spiders match the flowers where they lurk, waiting to ambush prey.

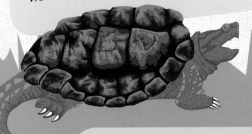

The cunning cougar stalks through the undergrowth ... and then pounces.

The scorpionfish has mottled skin to blend in with its coral habitat. It has toxic venom to paralyze prey.

The grouper's big-lipped mouth sucks in passing prey.

The cookiecutter shark ambushes prey bigger than itself. It bites cookie-sized chunks from its victim's flesh.

Some mantis shrimps dart out at prey as fast as 7.5 ft/s (2.3 m/s).

The chameleon is an artful ambusher. Its skin can change to be brown, green, blue, orange, or more.

An alligator looks like a floating log—until it rears from the water, and attacks.

SPINNER SHARKS HUNT IN SPIRALS

When fish shoals are threatened, they form a tight ball—but that doesn't put off the spinner shark!

TWISTY ATTACK

Spinner sharks make the most of the fish being all in one place. They spiral up through the "bait ball," snapping up fish. They spin so fast that they don't stop at the surface—they spin right up into the air!

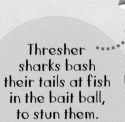

Thresher sharks bash their tails at fish in the bait ball, to stun them.

AFRICAN WILD DOGS
CAN OUT-HUNT LIONS

Fewer than a third of lion attacks end in a kill, but
African wild dogs have an 80% success rate!

AMAZING TEAMWORK

African wild dogs work together to surround a
herd of prey animals and separate off a weak
individual. They also take turns when it comes
to the chase, so no dog becomes too tired.

PACK RANK

An African wild dog pack contains
20 animals or more. The top breeding pair
are the leaders. However, they don't get
first pickings at a feast—youngsters do!

LEOPARDS KEEP
SECRET FOOD SUPPLIES

Like most big cats, the leopard hunts solo.

The leopard drags carcasses high into a tree to eat over a few days. This big cat eats prey of all sizes, from monkeys to baby giraffes. It is usually active at night and is a powerful swimmer, runner, and climber.

STEALTHY HUNTER

The leopard's rosette pattern helps it approach its prey without being noticed.

A male leopard can drag prey weighing 400 lb (180 kg) into a tree— that's three times its own weight!

HYENAS EAT LEFTOVERS

Hyenas are famous
for scavenging food from lion kills.

LAZY LEFTOVERS

Striped and brown hyenas feed mostly on carrion, but 95% of the spotted hyena's diet is meat that it has hunted and killed. Hyenas live and hunt or scavenge in packs. Thanks to their amazing, bone-crushing teeth, they eat every last bit of a carcass.

spotted
hyena

Striped and brown hyenas are both near threatened status.

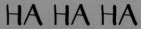
striped hyena

HA HA HA

Spotted hyenas are sometimes called laughing hyenas, because they make a creepy laughing noise. They are the most common large carnivores in Africa.

THE BIGGEST FISH EAT THE TINIEST FOOD

They eat plankton by filter-feeding—and there are two different methods.

basking shark

RAM FEEDERS

The basking shark swims open-mouthed through soupy plankton. Whenever it closes its mouth, water passes out of the gills and food goes down the throat. Manta rays and right whales feed this way, too.

SUCTION FEEDERS

Unlike the basking shark, whale sharks and megamouths actively suck in water. Then they pump it through their gills to separate the food. These sharks are suction feeders like humpbacks and big baleen whales.

megamouth

Caterpillars have
HUGE APPETITES

A caterpillar is an eating machine!

Caterpillars eat so much that their skin gets too tight. They have to shed their skin several times!

MUNCH, MUNCH

Caterpillars are the larvae (grubs) of butterflies and moths. They have strong jaws for munching. They eat constantly, sometimes doubling in size in just a few days.

FUNNY FOOD

Most caterpillars feed on plants. Others have more expensive tastes. Clothes moth caterpillars chomp through silks, wools, and other costly fabrics, ruining people's garments.

219

SOME BIRDS STOMP
SNAKES TO DEATH

The secretary bird is a very unusual bird of prey.

TERRESTRIAL TERROR

Most birds of prey hunt from the air, but the secretary bird spends most of its time on land. It is large and powerful, with muscular legs. It kills or paralyzes snakes and lizards by jumping on their backs over and over again.

TUCKING IN

The secretary bird tears up prey into bitesize chunks with its sharp talons. When it attacks smaller prey, such as insects, mice, and hares, it uses its bill, not its feet.

WOODPECKERS DRILL FOR DINNER

A woodpecker uses its sharp beak to peck at poles and trees.

A woodpecker can peck up to 20 times per second!

red-headed woodpecker

pileated woodpecker

long tongue for licking up sugary sap

FINDING FOOD

Holding out its stiff tail feathers for support, the woodpecker drills the wood to reach beetle grubs, other insects, and sap.

GREAT GRIP

Most woodpeckers have two toes that face forward and two that face back. It gives them a stronger grip than most birds, which usually have three forward-facing toes and one facing back.

The woodpecker's toes provide a strong grip.

221

FRIGATE BIRDS
ARE PIRATES

Frigate birds steal food from other seabirds.

AERIAL ATTACKER

Instead of diving for its own food, the frigate bird bullies another bird for its catch. When the bird drops its mouthful, the frigate bird swoops down and scoops it up.

A frigate bird can stay in the air for nearly two months. It eats and sleeps on the wing.

FLYING FISH

Frigate birds snap up another easy meal—flying fish. These fish jump out of the water to avoid dorado fish and other underwater predators.

MONKEYS USE NUTCRACKERS

Some macaques use stone tools to crack open nuts and shellfish.

LIFE BY THE SEA

The crab-eating macaque lives in lots of different habitats in Southeast Asia. In coastal areas, the monkey dives for crabs, sea snails, and oysters. It smashes the shells with a stone.

UP FOR ANYTHING

Macaques are omnivores—they eat plant food, meat, and fish. Fruit makes up a big part of their diet. They are also a pest, stealing sugarcane, sweet potatoes, and other crops from farms.

SMALL FISH FEED ON BIG ONES

Cleaner wrasses are small, busy reef fish that clean larger fish and turtles.

CLEANING STATIONS

Animals of the coral reef visit "cleaning stations" to be cleaned by the cleaner wrasses. Sometimes they even line up, waiting their turn. The little fish nibble off dead scales, slime, or parasites and their visitors leave looking clean and tidy!

CLEANER SHRIMPS

Wrasses aren't the only creatures that know how to get a free meal. Cleaner shrimp offer a similar service, even clambering about inside a predator's mouth.

ELECTRIC EELS
SHOCK THEIR PREY

These freshwater fish can produce their own electricity!

electric field

The electric eel lives in rivers and swamps in South America.

SIMPLY STUNNING

The electric eel has a long, eel-like body, but it is really a kind of knifefish. Its electricity-producing organs create an electric field around its body. It can release an 860-volt shock to stun its prey—usually crabs, lobsters, or crayfish.

FINDING FOOD

Only the electric eel sends out shocks, but all knifefish produce an electric field. They can sense if an animal enters and disturbs the electric field, which helps them to find prey.

MEERKATS SNACK ON SCORPIONS

Meerkats are not afraid of the sting in a scorpion's tail.

VARIED DIET

Meerkats belong to the mongoose family. Insects make up most of their diet, but they also eat fruit, eggs, and various animals, including snakes and scorpions.

REMOVING THE STING

The stinger at the end of a scorpion's tail pumps deadly venom into an attacker—but a meerkat won't give it the chance. It quickly bites off the scorpion's stinger then eats the rest of the creature at its leisure.

A meerkat isn't immune to venom—if a deadly scorpion manages to deliver a sting, the meerkat won't survive.

VULTURES ARE
BALD FOR A REASON

The vulture tucks into a meal headfirst.

DEAD MEAT

Vultures feed on carrion—rotten corpses. With no feathers on the head to get sticky and dirty, they can delve deep inside a big animal carcass.

HEAT CONTROL

Lack of head and neck feathers also helps the vulture to control its body temperature.

1 When it's hot, the vulture stretches its neck, exposing bare skin that loses heat.

2 When it's cold, the vulture hunches its body to expose less bare skin and keep in the heat.

227

BIG EATERS

The black rhino's diet includes more than 200 kinds of plant. White rhinos eat only grass.

Archerfish target insects on overhanging branches. They fire drops of water at them.

archerfish

Pangolins hunt at night for termites and ants. They swallow rocks to help digest them.

The duck-billed platypus doesn't have a stomach with acids to digest food. It breaks down food in the mouth by mashing it with gravel.

capybara

Capybaras live near rivers and lakes in South America. They gnaw reeds, grains, melons, and squash.

duck-billed platypus

Female horseflies have piercing mouthparts to suck blood from livestock and people. Males feed only on pollen and nectar.

redknee tarantula

The small-headed fly lays her eggs on a tarantula. When they hatch, the larvae eat the spider from the inside out.

The Indian grey mongoose fights cobras and eats them. It's resistant to small amounts of venom.

The giant isopod is a deep-sea crustacean. It can last for five years without eating.

Tigers mostly prey on deer, wild pigs, and buffalo. They will even eat baby elephants.

PIRANHAS AREN'T
BLOODTHIRSTY MANEATERS

There is even a vegetarian species of piranha!

The black piranha has the strongest bite force of any bony fish.

FEEDING FRENZY

Piranhas have a bad reputation. In times when food is scarce, one drop of blood in the water will attract schools of piranhas. The fish strip the carcass clean with their razor-sharp teeth.

OMNIVORES

Most of the time, piranhas eat plants, insects, snails, and smaller fish. They eat more seeds than meat! They don't pass up the opportunity if an easy meal falls into the water, but they rarely attack humans.

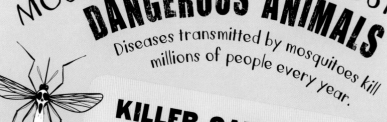

MOSQUITOES ARE THE MOST
DANGEROUS ANIMALS

Diseases transmitted by mosquitoes kill millions of people every year.

KILLER CARRIERS

The trouble is, mosquitoes can carry parasites, viruses, and bacteria. These microbes can enter a person's bloodstream when a mosquito feeds and cause disease.

THE GOOD NEWS

There are more than 3,500 types of mosquito, but only a couple species are primarily responsible for spreading disease.

THE BAD NEWS

One million people die of malaria each year.

OXPECKERS EAT EARWAX

The oxpecker is a bird with very strange eating habits!

GRAZING ON GRAZERS

The oxpecker lives in the African savanna. It picks ticks, lice, and maggots off large grazing animals. Its hosts include giraffes, antelope, buffalo, and rhinos.

BLOODSUCKERS!

Picking off parasites is helpful, but the oxpecker is a kind of parasite itself! It feeds on the host's earwax and skin. It even pecks open scabs to drink its host's blood.

There are two oxpecker species— red-billed and yellow-billed.

Oxpeckers pick hair off their hosts to line their nest holes.

SOME ANIMALS EAT THEIR OWN POOP

Rabbits, hares, and some rodents eat their own poop.

POOP-EATERS

Rabbit	Gopher
Guinea pig	Lemming
Hare	Vole
Chinchilla	Kangaroo rat

DOUBLE DIGESTION

These animals eat hard-to-digest stems and grasses. By gobbling freshly-made poop, they give their body a second chance to extract nutrients from a meal.

dung beetle

DUNG DIET

Some insects have a taste for poop. Flies and dung beetles lay their eggs in it, so that their babies hatch in a ready supply of food. Yummy!

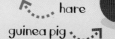
hare

guinea pig

lemming

233

FLAMINGOS AREN'T BORN PINK

Flamingo chicks are gray, not flamboyant pink!

WILD PIGMENTS

A flamingo's diet slowly turns its feathers orange or pink over time. It eats algae and shrimps, which contain natural dyes called carotenoids.

Humans eat carotenoids, too—they are found in carrots, sweet potatoes, tomatoes, and greens.

FISH TALES

Carotenoids are what give wild salmon healthy-looking, deep-pink flesh. Koi carp breeders deliberately feed carotenoids to their fish. It helps deepen their brilliant reds and oranges.

SEAFOOD TURNS
BOOBIES' FEET BLUE

The blue-footed booby is famous for its fabulous feet!

Dazzling dance

Male blue-footed boobies are so proud of their feet that they strut and dance to attract a mate. Females choose males with bright feet—for good reason.

SIGN OF HEALTH

Like the pink of the flamingo, the booby's blue feet are down to carotenoids. These pigments are in fish that the bird eats. The healthiest boobies have the bluest feet. Weaker ones need their carotenoids to build their immune system.

Booby chicks have white feet.

AGOUTIS CRACK BRAZIL NUTS

All rodents have strong teeth, but the agouti is a champion!

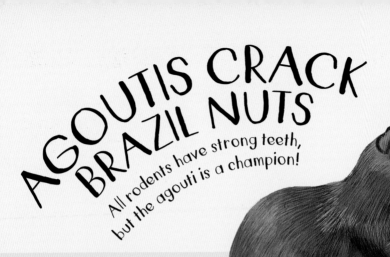

The agouti is a rain forest rodent, and is the only animal that feeds on brazil nuts. An extra layer of enamel strengthens its sharp teeth so it can crack the shells!

MACADAMIA MUNCHERS

The macadamia, which grows in Australia and New Zealand, is another hard nut with a protein-rich kernel. Rats climb trees to bore into the shells and steal the nuts.

Macaws raid macadamia plantations in South America—their beaks are strong enough to crack the shells.

ORANGUTANS EAT THE SMELLIEST FRUIT

The durian is the world's stinkiest fruit!

STRANGE FRUIT

The durian doesn't smell sweet like most fruit. It's more like a mix of pig poop, sweaty socks, and vomit! But many animals think it's the tastiest fruit—including orangutans, elephants, and even tigers!

ORANGUTAN MENU

flowers and bark

insects

leaves

fruit

Lots of fruit causes runny poops. Orangutans eat clay to stop this!

jackfruit

rambutans

durian

RED SQUIRRELS DRINK MAPLE SYRUP

These little rodents have a sweet tooth!

WINTER STORE

Red squirrels store up nuts and pinecones to eat over the winter, when food is scarce. What do they do if their stores run low? They harvest the sweet sap of the sugar maple tree.

TAPPING TECHNIQUE

We love maple syrup on pancakes or ice cream, but red squirrels slurp it straight from the tree! First they nibble a cut across the bark. Most of the sap drains away, but a lickable, sugary residue is left behind.

TREESHREWS DRINK ALCOHOL

The pen-tailed treeshrew drinks the equivalent of almost two bottles of wine a night.

pen-tailed treeshrew

FERMENTED NECTAR

The treeshrew feeds only on palm flower nectar. The nectar has fermented–its sugars have turned to alcohol–because of yeast that grows on the flower buds.

UNDER THE INFLUENCE

The treeshrew doesn't get drunk. Its body processes the alcohol so it cannot enter the bloodstream. Bohemian waxwings are not so lucky. These birds gobble up so many fermented rowanberries that they can't fly straight!

Bohemian waxwing

239

CHIMPS FISH FOR TERMITES

Chimpanzees use sticks as "fishing rods."

NEW AND IMPROVED!

Sometimes, the chimp runs its stick through its teeth first to give it a frayed, brushlike end. This design picks up more insects at once.

IT'S A CATCH

A chimp will carefully strip the leaves off a twig and poke it deep into a termite mound. It's a good way to extract juicy termites, which are too deep for the chimp to reach by hand.

Chimps use stone tools, too—just like their cousins, macaques and capuchin monkeys.

240

SNEAKY MANTISES
LOOK LIKE FLOWERS

Some praying mantises mimic flowers to trick prey.

SLOW MOVER

The praying mantis is a large, predatory insect that feeds on beetles and other insects. Its hunting technique is to stay very still and then ambush prey.

A praying mantis is named for how it holds its front legs—as if its "hands" are together in prayer!

orchid mantis

Matching mantises

Many mantises are green, to blend in with leaves. Others are white, pink, or yellow to match the flowers where they wait.

DEFENSIVE CAMOUFLAGE

The pygmy seahorse is almost impossible to spot. It's tiny, and looks like its pink coral habitat.

The leafy sea dragon is another well-disguised seahorse. Its fins sway like fronds of seaweed.

Walking sticks or stick insects are green or brown. Their thin bodies mimic branches.

leafy sea dragon

Leaf costumes are a great disguise. The leaf-tailed gecko is a master.

Many polar animals are white. The Arctic owl's pale feathers hide it from foxes and wolves.

Arctic owl

242

Many female ducks have dull feathers. It stops predators spying them or their nest.

Flounders are well camouflaged against a sandy or pebbly seabed.

A mossy frog's bumpy green skin looks just like moss.

A pheasant's feathers blend in with the ground, soil, and leaves.

flounder

pheasant

The bittern's a wetland bird. When it stands still, beak pointing skyward, it could be mistaken for a reed!

The leaf frog is almost invisible in leaf litter. It resembles an old leaf.

leaf frog

243

ANTEATERS HAVE LONG TONGUES

An anteater's tongue is super-long and super-stretchy.

Snouty slurper

The anteater's appearance is strange enough before it opens its mouth, thanks to its long, narrow snout. However, its weirdest feature is its flexible tongue, designed for slurping up ants.

SPEED-LICKING

A giant anteater is 7 ft (2.1 m) long—and its narrow, spine-covered tongue is a whopping 2 ft (0.6 m)! It flicks in and out of an anthill up to 160 times per minute. The anteater works quickly to avoid being bitten by the ants.

Anteaters don't have any teeth.

SNOW MONKEYS WASH THEIR FOOD
Japanese macaques use sea or river water to rinse food.

CLEVER MONKEY

It all started when a female monkey had the bright idea of washing the soil off her food. Before long, the rest of the troop was copying her!

SURVIVING SNOW

The Japanese macaque is nicknamed the "snow monkey" because its home, in northern Japan, is snow-covered for much of the year. That doesn't bother the monkeys, though—they keep warm by bathing in hot springs.

Snow monkeys live in a colder climate than any other primate—except humans!

PANDAS ARE PICKY EATERS

Bears might like a varied diet, but not giant pandas!

POOR DIET

Around 99 percent of the panda's diet is bamboo, but it isn't very nourishing. A panda must eat up to 84 lb (38 kg) of bamboo every day.

PANDAS IN DANGER

There are only 1,864 pandas left in the wild. Their bamboo forest habitat is being cut down.

Pandas have evolved an extra sixth digit or "thumb." They use it to grasp bamboo stems.

SOME ANIMALS GO MONTHS WITHOUT EATING

Crocodiles can last
over a year without a meal.

Crocodiles
appeared
ten million years
before the first
dinosaurs.

SURVIVORS!

In the 240 million years that crocodiles
have been on the planet, they've seen
some tough times. They often go
without food for a few months,
but if necessary they can
survive for over a year.

American crocodile

Nile crocodile

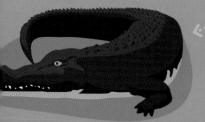

SAVING ENERGY

Crocodiles don't use much energy.
They hardly move and they don't
make their own body heat.

247

STRANGE DIETS

Tear-drinking moths and bees that poke an animal's eye to make it cry.

A tiger salamander will eat its own brothers and sisters.

tiger salamander

The vampire squid feeds on so-called "marine snow"–all the flakes of dead stuff that float down toward the seabed.

The skua is a seabird. It will attack a seagull till it throws up, then eat the gull's vomit.

skua

The vampire finch is named for its habit of sucking the blood of booby birds.

The ommatokoita is a parasite. It feeds on the eye of the Greenland shark.

Tiger shark pups eat their brothers and sisters while they are still in the womb.

Carrion beetles bury corpses. Once underground, they create food for baby beetles.

Cows' food returns to their mouth from their stomach for a second chew.

Cockchafer beetles lay their eggs in soil. Their larvae feed on plant roots.

BEETLES CAN CHOMP THROUGH HOUSES

Some beetles eat wood!

carpet
beetle

WOODWORM

Powderpost beetles, deathwatch beetles, house longhorns, and furniture beetles are just some of the culprits. Their larvae, known as woodworm, spend years eating through floorboards, joists, and furniture.

powderpost
beetle

NO MATERIAL IS SAFE

Insect pests also eat clothes and carpets. Clothes moths and carpet beetles munch through silk, fur, cotton, and wool.

clothes moth

Deathwatch beetles tap on wood to attract a mate. People used to say the spooky sound meant death was on its way.

WEEVILS ARE VERY BORING!

Weevils have super-long snouts for "boring" into plants.

Specialist feeders

Weevils belong to the beetle family. Most feed on one kind of plant. The acorn weevil drills into acorns and the nut weevil into hazelnuts. Boll weevils eat cotton buds and flowers, grain weevils attack grain, and red palm weevils feed on coconut and date palms.

red palm weevil

In parts of Southeast Asia, people eat red palm weevil grubs as a special treat.

giraffe weevil

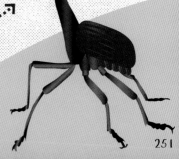

CRAZY NECK!

Male giraffe weevils' snouts are especially long! They joust each other with them.

SLIME PUTS OFF PREDATORS

Many creatures produce defensive slime.

hagfish

hagfish slime

THE BLOB

Hagfish have a disgusting habit. They ooze slime if they sense a fish about to attack. It's a great strategy because the slime clogs up the attacker's gills, and it soon backs off!

SUPER GLUE

Amphibians are usually moist, but one salamander takes slime to a new level. When a slimy salamander feels threatened, it produces mucus. The gloop glues up the predator's paws.

armadillo

A BALL'S A SAFE SHAPE

Some animals curl up to defend themselves.

Even a lion can't get its teeth into a pangolin when it's in a ball.

pangolin

ROUND AND ROUND

Armadillos and pangolins live on different continents, but they both curl up if a predator approaches, and both have protective, scaly plates to defend themselves.

trilobite

BALL DEFENDERS

The first animals to defend themselves by rolling up were sea creatures called trilobites, millions of years ago. Their living relatives, woodlice, use the same technique.

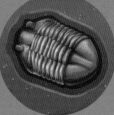

253

LIONS ARE THE ONLY CATS THAT AREN'T LONERS

Lions live together in family groups called prides.

PRIDE NUMBERS

A pride has related females, their cubs, and a few adult males. The lionesses do the hunting. As a team, they can take down larger or speedier prey than they could alone, but they also have to share the kill.

Young males leave the pride by the age of three.

SHRINKING POPULATION

Today, wild lions live only in sub-Saharan Africa and India. In prehistoric times, they prowled across Europe and North and South America.

SWANS MATE FOR LIFE

Like many birds, swans usually stick with one partner.

COURTSHIP RITUALS

Swans choose their mate at the age of four or five. Mute swan couples twist their graceful necks into a heart shape. Trumpeter swans honk loudly when they pair off.

PRACTICE MAKES PERFECT

Swans usually stay together till they die—at around age 20. Each year they raise a new clutch of cygnets, and each year they improve the survival rate of the new clutch.

LIFETIME LOVERS

Turtle doves

Lovebirds

Hornbills

Black vultures

Bald eagles

black widow

BLACK WIDOWS EAT THEIR MATES

After mating, many black widow spiders make a meal of their partner.

A NOURISHING START

It might sound harsh, but the female takes in vital proteins when she eats the male. The extra nourishment gives her eggs and spiderlings the best possible start in life.

Australian redbacks are close cousins of black widows.

Australian redback

MATE... THEN DIE!

Many spider females are cannibals. A male Australian redback actually somersaults into his partner's mouth! A male dark fishing spider dies after mating so that his partner can eat him.

256

HORNBILLS HAVE THEIR CHICKS IN PRISON

A female hornbill stays trapped in her nest hole for 5 months.

Hornbills do not break open their nest hole until the chicks are big enough to leave.

great hornbill

TRAPPED!

The hornbill nests in a hole in a tree. Sitting inside, she slowly seals up the hole until only a tiny slit is left. The male brings her building materials and food. The female cannot get out—but no predator can get in!

BUILDING MATERIALS

✓ mud

✓ regurgitated food

✓ droppings

ANGLERFISH FATHERS ARE TINY

The anglerfish lives in the vast, deep ocean, where it's hard to find a mate.

BECOMING ONE

In some anglerfish, the male is much smaller than the female. When he finds a female, he clings on by his teeth. Over time, his body merges with hers. He loses his eyes and organs and becomes a parasite.

A fishing rod "lure" sticks out over the female anglerfish's mouth. Its glowing tip brings prey close.

GIVE AND TAKE

One female anglerfish can have more than six attached males. Her body supports and feeds them. In return, they fertilize her eggs.

MALE ELEPHANT SEALS ARE TWICE AS BIG AS FEMALES

A southern elephant seal bull weighs up to 4.5 tons (4 tonnes).

BIG AND BLUBBERY

Southern elephant seals live around the Southern Ocean. Being large keeps them warm in cold seas and on harsh coasts. Males are twice as long as females—and weigh up to eight times more!

NOISY DADDY

The male elephant seal's trunklike nose makes his snorts, grunts, and bellows super-loud. The top, or dominant, bull in the colony mates with all the females.

male

female

Elephant seals can stay underwater for up to two hours.

FIGHTING MALES

Rattlesnakes don't have territory. They decide who mates with the females by having wrestling matches.

Male stag beetles do battle with their outsize jaws, which look like stag's antlers.

Sheep and goats have headbutting contests to decide which male is the best.

It's the female topi antelopes, not the males, who fight over a mate!

bighorn sheep

Pikas are mountain mammals, related to rabbits and hares. Rather than have physical fights, the males chase and taunt each other.

Male rhinoceros beetles use their rhino-like horn to fight other males.

cardinal bird

From kingfishers to cardinals, many male birds have fierce fights over territory. They need it to attract a female.

Fighting male moose lock their enormous antlers, which can be 6 ft (1.8 m) across.

Male gorillas usually decide who's dominant with hoots and chest-beating displays. If they do fight, it's to the death.

A male hippo's toothy yawn is a sign of aggression. It means "back off—or prepare for a vicious fight!"

ZEBRA STALLIONS
NECK-WRESTLE

When a zebra male is challenged, a battle begins.

Like zebras, wild horses never fight to the death. The loser always backs down.

ZEBRA COMBAT

1 The zebras circle each other warily. Eventually they both kneel down to protect their legs.

2 They shuffle around on their knees, trying to bite each other.

3 They neck-wrestle, slamming into each other neck-first.

4 They scramble to their feet and attack. They bite and kick viciously until the loser gallops off.

KANGAROOS ARE CHAMPION KICKBOXERS

Kangaroos use their "arms" to keep their distance—the real fighting happens with the feet.

KANGAROO KICKS

Male kangaroos sense when a female is ready to mate. They might have to fight off a rival first. Kangaroos can deliver powerful kicks.

POUCH PROTECTION

The female kangaroo has her baby a month after mating. The grape-sized newborn crawls to her pouch and develops there for up to ten months.

A newborn and a youngster (joey) can share the same pouch. The mother gives them different milk.

Sea horse fathers
GIVE BIRTH

The sea horse is the only animal where the male becomes pregnant!

PREGNANT POUCH

A male sea horse has a pouch on his body. The female lays her eggs inside and he fertilizes them. The male carries the developing eggs, and gives them oxygen and food.

SMALL FRY!

Small sea horse species have 50 to 150 babies at a time, but larger ones produce up to 2,000! Only about 5 in a thousand of the babies, called fry, survive to have their own young. Sea horses are poor swimmers, but they can grip seagrass with their tails so the tide doesn't sweep them away.

SOME PENGUINS ARE
STAY-AT-HOME FATHERS

The female emperor penguin lays a single egg, which she gives to her mate to keep warm.

BALANCING ACT

The males huddle together for warmth, balancing their precious eggs on their feet so they do not touch the ice.

FEASTING FEMALES

Each female heads off to sea for eight weeks to fill up on krill, fish, and squid. She returns just before her chick hatches. She provides its first meal by vomiting up partly-digested food. Yum!

265

A GIANT CLAM SQUIRTS
OUT A BILLION EGGS

Giant clams are huge—more than 4.5 ft (135 cm) long.

Clouds of eggs

An adult giant clam's body is cemented to a coral reef, so it cannot travel to find a mate. Instead, it releases clouds of eggs and sperm into the water. All the nearby clams do the same.

A giant clam can live for a century or more.

MIXING GENES

Animals that make both eggs and sperm are called hermaphrodites. Like the giant clam, most cross-fertilize—sperm from another animal fertilizes their eggs.

About 65,000 animal species are hermaphrodites.

266

SOME MAMMALS LAY EGGS

The duck-billed platypus is one of the oddest mammals.

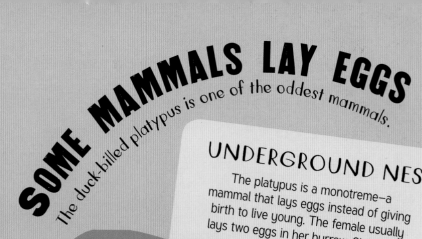

UNDERGROUND NEST

The platypus is a monotreme—a mammal that lays eggs instead of giving birth to live young. The female usually lays two eggs in her burrow. She keeps them warm until they hatch.

MOTHER'S MILK

Newly hatched platypus babies are bald and helpless. They drink milk, but their mother doesn't have nipples—the milk drips from her pores.

Echidnas are the only other egg-laying mammals.

ALL ABOUT EGGS

Snowy owl eggs have thick shells to keep out the UV rays of the Arctic sun.

Storm petrels' eggs can survive the Alaskan cold while their parents are away looking for food.

storm petrels

Horn sharks' eggs are in spiral-shaped egg cases. They screw them into gaps in the rocks.

Mermaids' purses are the washed-up empty egg cases of skates and dogfish.

skate egg case

The vervain hummingbird's egg is less than 0.4 in (1 cm) long.

The ostrich lays 7–10 eggs at a time. It has the largest eggs—the record weight was 5.7 lb (2.6 kg).

ostrich egg

chicken egg

Hoopoes cover their eggs with sticky, stinky brown slime. It contains bacteria that protect the eggs from infections.

hoopoes

A cichlid mother stores developing eggs in her mouth for up to a month, till the fish are fully-formed fry.

A male midwife toad carries eggs on his back until they are just about to hatch.

Baby whale sharks develop in egg capsules inside the female's body. Each capsule is more than 23.6 in (60 cm) across.

foam-nest frog

African foam-nest frogs lay eggs in meringue-like foam on branches over ponds. The tadpoles drop into the water when they're developed.

SNAKES CAN GIVE BIRTH TO UP TO 50 BABIES

Not all snakes lay eggs—some give birth to live young.

boa constrictor

INSIDE EGGS

Snakes from cooler climates usually produce live babies. Baby rattlesnakes and vipers develop inside eggs in the mother's body, then hatch as live young. The egg has a yolk to nourish them.

More than two-thirds of snakes lay eggs.

yellow anaconda

VIVIPAROUS SNAKES

Boas, anacondas, and many sea snakes don't develop in eggs at all. As they develop, their mother feeds them through a placenta. Boas have from 15 to 50 snakelings!

BABY TURTLES
RACE FOR THEIR LIVES

A newly hatched turtle must dash down the beach, avoiding predators.

Turtle eggs are soft and round, with a leathery "shell."

Turtle eggs

A female sea turtle lays her eggs on the beach where she was born. She comes ashore at night, scrapes a shallow nest, lays 80 to 120 eggs, covers them with sand, then returns to the sea.

PERILOUS PATH

Two months later, the turtle hatchlings dig through the sand to the surface. During their scramble to the sea, some are eaten by crabs and birds, while others are baked alive in the sun.

271

A RABBIT HAS 1,000 KITS IN A LIFETIME

A rabbit only lives for 12 years, but it produces a lot of kits (babies) in that time.

READY TO MATE

A female rabbit (doe) is fully grown at three months. After mating, she is pregnant for a month before she gives birth to her first litter of 5 to 12 kits.

A doe is pregnant non-stop through spring, summer, and autumn. She has a break over the winter.

HUNGRY KITS

For the first three weeks, kits feed only on milk. Then they start to nibble grass, too, and their mother is free to feed her next litter.

Armadillos have
IDENTICAL QUADRUPLETS

Armadillos are the only mammals—apart from humans—that consistenly have identical babies.

EGG SPLIT

A nine-banded armadillo mother produces only one egg, but it splits into four as it develops. Each becomes a separate but identical baby. Each has exactly the same DNA.

A frightened nine-banded armadillo can leap 4 ft (122 cm) into the air!

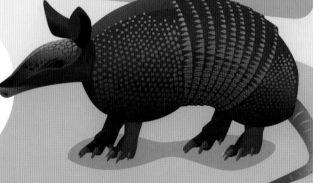

LIFE WITH MOTHER

Armadillo babies live with their mother in her burrow for at least a year. Over her lifetime, a female nine-banded armadillo has up to 56 young.

KOALA JOEYS EAT POOP CALLED PAP!

Pap helps a young koala move from milk to eucalyptus.

Eucalyptus contains toxins that are poisonous to most mammals, but not koalas.

POUCH LIFE

Like a kangaroo, a newborn koala is tiny and undeveloped. It crawls into its mother's pouch, attaches to a teat, and continues to grow. At around six months old, it starts to feed on pap as well as milk.

Runny, mushy poop

Ordinary koala poop is hard and dry but pap is runny. It passes important microbes from the mother to the joey. The youngster needs these to digest eucalyptus leaves.

CROCODILES
are devoted mothers
Many reptiles abandon their
eggs, but not crocodiles.

TEMPERATURE IS KEY

The crocodile lays her
eggs in a mound
of vegetation
and pees on the
mound to warm it!
If the temperature in
the nest is 89–94 °F (31.7–
34.7 °C), the baby crocodiles will be
male. Any cooler or hotter and the
babies will be female.

NEW LIFE

When they are ready to
hatch, the crocodiles call
from their eggs. Their
mother comes and clears
away the nest mound. She
carries the hatchlings
to the water in her
tooth-lined mouth!

A crocodile
lays 35–50
eggs.

BABY PANDAS AREN'T
BLACK AND WHITE

A newborn panda cub looks pink!

SHADING IN

Newborn pandas have a fine covering of white hair—so fine that the pink of their skin shows through. From about a week old, patches of black fur grow around the eyes, ears, and shoulders.

TINY TOT

Apart from pouched mammals, such as koalas and kangaroos, panda mothers have the smallest mammal babies relative to their own size. A newborn panda weighs just 3-5 oz (85-142 g).

Dalmatian dogs are prized for their black spots, but their puppies are usually born pure white!

SUNFISH BABIES WEAR STAR-SHAPED SUITS

Adult sunfish look weird—but their offspring look weirder!

BIG AND ROUND

The ocean sunfish looks like a big blob! Weighing up to 2,205 lb (1,000 kg), it's the heaviest bony fish. It spends a lot of its time floating near the surface, sunbathing.

An ocean sunfish produces up to 300 million eggs per season—more than any vertebrate.

SHAPE SHIFTING

Surprisingly, the sunfish has tiny eggs that hatch into pinhead-sized larvae. The larvae have a transparent, star-shaped case. Fry—the next life stage—have spines, like puffer fish.

277

TAPIR CALVES LOOK
NOTHING
LIKE THEIR PARENTS

A baby tapir has crazy stripes and spots.

Tapirs have horselike hooves and piglike snouts.

CUTE CAMOUFLAGE

The pattern on a young tapir's coat helps to camouflage it in the dappled light of the forest. The markings fade by about six months old.

ADULT APPEARANCES

Tapirs in South America are dark brown all over as adults. The Malayan tapir has a white "saddle" around its middle. It's the largest tapir species.

SOME FROGS CHANGE SHADE AS THEY GROW

Many frogs alter as they age, but none as much as Ezra's cross frog!

WARNING

Ezra's cross frog lives in Papua New Guinea. The froglet is black with yellow spots. It looks like a poison-dart frog! Scientists aren't sure why, but the mature frog doesn't have these warning spots. It is pure peach!

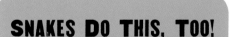

SNAKES DO THIS, TOO!

An adult green tree python hunts in the trees and blends in with the leaves. But as a youngster, it is bright yellow or red. It can hide better among the flowers, where it preys on small lizards.

PELICANS SERVE CHICKS
FOOD IN A BAG

A pelican chick eats fish from the pouch under its parent's beak.

READY MEALS

Many birds "vomit out" (regurgitate) food for chicks. The food is easy to eat because it is already partly digested. Pelicans are fish-eaters, so their chicks eat fish. Chicks of garden birds eat worms, caterpillars, or beetles.

The chick that makes the most noise receives the most food!

PESTER POWER

Baby birds pester their parents for food with cheeps, calls, or screeches, and by showing off the bright insides of their mouths.

SOME BABIES EAT
THEIR OWN MOTHERS

For some spiderlings, the mother is the first meal on the menu!

SELF SACRIFICE

A mother desert spider spews out her stomach contents for her young. Then she digests her own insides so her young can eat. Other selfless arachnid mothers include crab spiders and pseudoscorpions.

Baby earwigs eat their mother if food is scarce.

SKIN STRIPPERS

Caecilians are wormlike amphibians that live underground. Sometimes youngsters snack on strips of their mother's skin. Luckily for her, it grows back!

crab spider

281

SEAL MILK IS THE CREAMIEST

A harp seal's milk is 12 times creamier than a cow's milk.

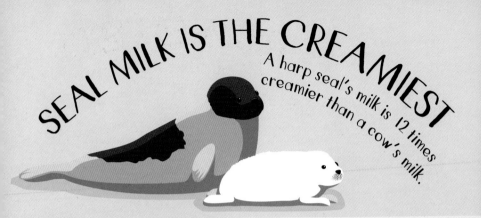

GROW FAST

Harp seal pups are born in the icy Arctic. Their mother nurses them with her energy-rich milk. The pups grow quickly. At three weeks they begin to use their fluffy white fur.

Bird "milk"

Pigeons, flamingos, and emperor penguins feed their chicks crop milk–fatty liquid produced in their crop (throat pouch).

BABY DART FROGS EAT EGGS

Strawberry poison-darts serve up eggs to their tadpoles.

BRINGING UP BABY

1 The father guards the eggs until they hatch.

2 The mother carries each tadpole to a different bromeliad plant.

3 For six weeks, the mother produces unfertilized eggs for the tadpoles.

Poison-dart tadpoles are cannibals. That's why the parents raise them in separate pools!

SUPER-FOOD

The eggs give the tadpoles vital proteins and other nourishment. They also contain the dangerous poisons that protect poison-dart frogs from predators.

CRAZY ANIMAL BABIES

The largest litter of kittens was 19, born to a Burmese-Siamese crossbreed.

One naked mole-rat litter was a record-breaking 33 pups.

A mother tiger usually has three or four cubs. Sometimes she has a record litter of seven, but if this happens, four or five won't survive.

A kiwi chick hatches from an egg that is 20% of its mother's own weight!

kiwi

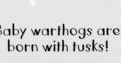

Baby warthogs are born with tusks!

Some baby hippos are born underwater. Their mother pushes them to the surface to take their first breath.

A blue whale calf is the biggest baby—it weighs about 3 tons (2.7 tonnes) when it's born!

Madagascar's tailless tenrec usually gives birth to 15 babies at a time.

Elephant calves drink their mother's milk for up to four years.

Echidna babies are called puggles. They have no hairs and no spines!

PARENT BIRDS FAKE BROKEN WINGS

Some birds put on an act to protect their offspring from predators.

DISTRACTING DISPLAY

Plovers nest on the ground. The mother bird will do anything to keep her chicks safe. If a hunter comes near, she limps away from the nest, dragging her wing. The predator moves after her—and away from the babies!

plover

sandpiper

OTHER BROKEN WING FAKERS

Sandpiper

Avocet

Snipe

Oystercatcher

Some ground-nesters sit on a decoy "nest," a little distance from the real one.

CHEETAH MOTHERS
ARE ALWAYS MOVING HOUSE
A cheetah moves her cubs every few days.

HOME ALONE

The cheetah raises her cubs on her own. To produce milk to feed them, she must eat—and that means going hunting and leaving the cubs. It's risky, because lions and hyenas prey on baby cheetahs.

Only five percent of cheetah cubs survive the first year of life.

TOOTHY TRANSPORT

To lessen the risk of her babies being found, the cheetah keeps changing her den. She carries the cubs in her mouth by the scruff of the neck.

287

SCORPIONS CARRY BABIES ON THEIR BACK

The scorpion defends her young with the sting in her tail.

WELCOME TO THE WORLD

A scorpion mother has up to 100 babies at once. They don't hatch from eggs like spiders— they are born alive, and crawl onto her back.

A scorpion can inject venom from the stinger at the end of its tail.

SCORPION SAFETY

The mother carries the babies around for two or three weeks. Their outer casing, or exoskeleton, is still soft. Once it's hardened up, the young scorpions can climb down and live on their own.

GREBE CHICKS HITCH A RIDE

Grebes are water birds. They build floating nests.

FREE RIDE

Newly hatched grebe chicks sit on their mother's back as she glides around the pond or lake. They are stripy and hard to spot. The father swims alongside. He dives for fish and feeds them to the chicks.

GREAT RED SPOT

Each grebe chick has a bald spot on its head, above its beak. The spot reddens as the chick begs for food. The spot fades when the chick's been fed. It's a pushy sign that says to the parent "feed me!"

NOT ALL DUCKLINGS HAVE DUCK PARENTS

When they hatch, ducklings follow the first moving thing they see!

READY TO GO

Goslings and ducklings hatch able to waddle and swim. They are programmed to follow their mother. This is called imprinting.

FAITHFUL FOLLOWERS

Imprinting is nature's way of making sure goslings and ducklings stick together and stay safe. If there is no mother around, the orphaned chicks might imprint on another animal or even a human.

A couple of days after hatching, goslings and ducklings can no longer imprint. If they see something larger than them, their reaction now is fear!

GLOVE PUPPETS
FEED CHICKS

Puppets are pretend parents in breeding programs.

Survival plan

Cranes are wetland birds. Siberian and whooping cranes are just two species in danger of dying out. When chicks are bred in captivity, they have more chance of survival—but they need to be able to fit in with a real flock when they're released.

In 1941, there were just 21 whooping cranes left in the wild. Today there are around 600 birds.

PUPPET POWER

Workers on breeding programs wear crane glove puppets when they feed the chicks. They want the chicks to keep their natural trust of cranes and fear of humans.

MUSK OXEN FORM FORTS AROUND THEIR CALVES

Musk oxen are large, shaggy-haired animals.

An adult musk ox stands around 5 ft (1.5 m) at the shoulder.

TUNDRA DANGER

Herds of musk oxen live in the Arctic. Wolves and other predators could attack their calves, especially when they are newborn. The herd works together to protect the young.

WALL OF PROTECTION

In times of danger, musk oxen form a defensive circle around the youngest, oldest, and weakest members of the herd. Any predator is faced by a wall of sturdy beasts with long, curved horns.

WILDEBEEST RUN AT FIVE MINUTES OLD

Some antelope calves hide from predators, but wildebeest babies are born ready to run.

SCRAMBLE TO SURVIVE

Also known as gnus, wildebeest are large antelopes that live in herds on African grasslands. They're constantly on the move for fresh grazing. Their calves scramble to their feet within minutes of being born—if they don't, they'll be left behind.

THREATS TO CALVES

Spotted hyenas

Cheetahs

Lions

Leopards

Crocodiles

Predators pick off between a fifth and half of young wildebeest. Bigger herds have higher survival rates.

293

LION CUBS MUST PLAY

Games are a serious business for many young mammals.

SUPER SKILLS

When lion cubs pounce, prowl, and wrestle, they're not just having fun. They are learning the skills they'll need as adults. They learn basic motor skills—how to move—and improve their coordination. They build up their strength.

MIND GAMES

Play also gives the cubs' brains a workout, which helps their mental development. Interacting with each other teaches them the social skills that they'll need for living in a pride.

There are usually two or three lion cubs in a litter.

AXOLOTLS NEVER GROW UP

Most amphibians grow legs and move onto land, but not the axolotl.

GILLS TO LUNGS

The axolotl is a salamander from Mexico. All salamanders hatch from eggs in water. Like tadpoles, they have gills to breathe underwater. Like frogs, most salamanders lose their gills, develop lungs, and live on land as adults.

LAKE LIFE

The axolotl lives its whole life in the water. It keeps its feathery gills and its tail fin and stays in its lake home. It feeds on worms, insect larvae, mollusks, and even fish.

Most axolotls are mottled brown or black, but some are white, pink, or golden.

ADULT MAYFLIES LIVE FOR
FEWER THAN FIVE MINUTES

A mayfly nymph lives for years, but its adult life lasts just days, hours, or even minutes.

There are more than 2,000 different mayfly species.

UNDERWATER LIFE

The mayfly lays its eggs in fresh water. The larvae, or nymphs, eat algae for up to three years. When the mayfly finally comes out of the water, it leaves behind its old exoskeleton.

LIFE GOES ON

The mayfly's new, adult form has wings. The insect takes to the air, mates, and dies. If it's a female, it drops its eggs into the water first, and the cycle begins again.

mayfly nymph

SOME ANIMALS LIVE FOREVER

A few species of jellyfish are immortal —able to go on living forever!

immortal jellyfish

LIFE OF A JELLYFISH

A jellyfish usually goes through five life stages—egg, planula, polyp, larva, and medusa (adult jellyfish). When medusas release sperm and eggs into the water, the life cycle starts again with each fertilized egg.

HAPPILY EVER AFTER

The immortal jellyfish has a neat trick that means it can live forever. If it's sick, old, or wounded, it turns back into a polyp. From here it buds into new larvae and grows into new medusas—on and on forever!

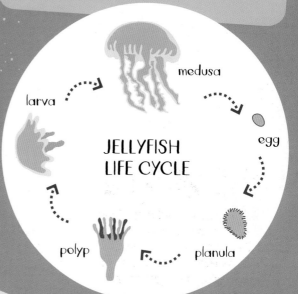

JELLYFISH LIFE CYCLE

medusa

egg

planula

polyp

larva

INDEX

agoutis 236
albatrosses 17, 88
alpacas 46
anglerfish 258
anteaters 244
ants 57, 95, 113
Arctic foxes 74
armadillos 253, 273
axolotls 299

badgers 111
barnacles 86
bats 5, 32, 69, 176
beaks 23
bears 77, 205
beavers 92
bees 115, 140, 180
beetles 134, 165, 249, 250
big cats 8
birds 7, 18, 78, 94,
  96–97, 104, 117, 286
birds of prey 104, 117, 220
black smokers 89
bones 18–19
bowerbirds 195
breathing
  34–35, 71

burrows 102–103
butterflies 16, 140,
  150, 298

camels 40, 126–127
camouflage 242–243, 279
caribou 149
caterpillars 219
cats 45, 170
caves 68–69, 161
chameleons 29
cheetahs 8, 105, 287
chimpanzees 12, 240
clams 130, 266
clownfish 91
cockroaches 115, 140
coral reefs 36, 90
crabs 10, 101, 147, 161
cranes 291
crocodiles 28, 122,
  247, 275
cuttlefish 144

deer 51, 60, 65
deserts 78–79
dinosaurs 133
dogs 43, 44, 176, 215
dolphins 26, 185
donkeys 126

dragonflies 85, 112, 156
ducks 65, 290

eagles 80, 96
earthworms 51, 138, 163
echidnas 47, 285
eels 153, 225
eggs 265, 266–271,
  273, 283
elephants 25,
  82, 124, 126,
  175, 285
emus 127
Etruscan shrews 5
exoskeletons 14
eyes 154–157,
  160–161, 166–171

falcons 96, 104
farm animals 72–73
feathers 27, 196, 197
fighting 260–263
fireflies 186
fish 36–37, 65,
  118, 161, 224
flamingos 234
fleas 121
flies 85, 140, 165
flight 17, 18, 112, 117

flocks 114
forests 60–61
foxes 33, 62, 74
freshwater animals 84–85
frigate birds 222
frogs 34, 59, 84, 110,
  181, 187, 269, 279, 283
fur 26–27, 74

geckos 137
gibbons 108
giraffes 19, 48
goats 70, 125
gorillas 13, 261
grasslands 64
grebes 289

habitats 54, 88
hermit crabs 101
herons 87
hippos 66, 124, 261, 285
hornbills 257
horses 106
hoverflies 191
hummingbirds 7, 23, 99
hyenas 217

insects 14, 112, 114–115,
  134, 140–141, 164–165,
  233, 250–251
invertebrates 15

jaguars 123
jaws 22

jellyfish 209, 301

kangaroos 120, 263
kiwis 173
koalas 49, 274
komodo dragons 211
kookaburras 202

lemurs 13, 109
leopards 216
lions 254, 294
lizards 50, 59, 136,
  188, 192, 211

macaques 63, 223, 245
mammals 5, 267
mammoths 83
manatees 178
mantises 241
mayflies 300
meerkats 102, 226
mice 182
migration 146–153
millipedes 21
mockingbirds 200
moles 162, 172
monkeys 11, 63, 108,
  198–199, 223, 245
mosquitoes
  194, 231
mudskippers 118
musk oxen 292

nests 94–99

octopuses 190
olms 68
orangutans
  13, 237
orcas 204
ostriches 6, 135, 268
otters 142
owls 167
oxpeckers 232

pandas 246, 276
pangolins 228, 253
parrots 45, 201
pearls 53
pelicans 280
penguins 143, 265
pets 44–45
pigeons 63, 104
piranhas 230
platypuses 228, 267
polar bears 75
prairie dogs 79
primates 12–13
puffer fish 193

rabbits 272
rain forests 56–59

rats 63
rays 116
regrowing 51
rhinos 41, 124
rodents 24, 233

salmon 152
scales 27, 42
scallops 145
scorpions 226, 288
sea horses 264
seals 179, 197, 259, 282
secretary birds 220
servals 9
sharks 28, 38, 154, 166,
    174, 214, 218, 248
sheep 70
sifakas 109
skin 26–27, 42, 75
sleep 48–49, 77
sloths 49, 58
slow lorises 131
slugs 139
smell, sense of 172–175
snails 139, 160, 208
snakes 22, 31, 42, 119,
    155, 158, 188, 206–207,
    210, 270, 279
snow leopards 76
spiders 30, 52, 171,
    196, 212, 256, 281
squid 168

squirrels 24, 79, 238
starfish (sea stars) 20, 51
storks 87
sunfish 39, 277
swans 255
swarms 114–115

tails 50
tamarins 295
tapirs 278
tarsiers 169
teeth 24
termites 93, 296
thorny devils 81
tiger beetles 134
tigers 8, 229, 284
toads 110
tortoises 132
transport 126–127
treeshrews 239
turtles 100, 151, 212, 271

vultures 227

walruses 203
warthogs 128
wasps 98, 164, 191
water buffalo 127

weaver ants 95
weaver birds 94
weevils 251
whales 4, 35, 67,
    148, 184, 204
wildebeest 293
wolverines 61
wolves 183
woodpeckers 221
worms 138, 163, 297
wrasses 224

yaks 71

zebras 262